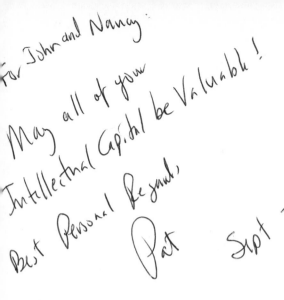

For John and Nancy:

May all of your
Intellectual Capital be Valuable!

Best Personal Regards,

Pat

Sept 2000

W9-BRP-105

Value-Driven
Intellectual Capital

Value-Driven Intellectual Capital

How to Convert Intangible Corporate Assets Into Market Value

Patrick H. Sullivan

John Wiley & Sons, Inc.

New York • Chichester • Weinheim • Brisbane • Singapore • Toronto

Library of Congress Cataloging-in-Publication Data:
Sullivan, Patrick H.
  Value-driven intellectual capital : how to convert intangible
corporate assets into market value / Patrick H. Sullivan.
      p.   cm. — (Intellectual property series)
    Includes bibliographical references and index.
    ISBN 0-471-35104-0 (cloth : alk. paper)
    1. Intellectual capital—Management.   2. Intellectual property.
  3. Knowledge management.   I. Title.   II. Series: Intellectual
property series (John Wiley & Sons)
  HD53.S85   2000
  658.4'038—dc21   99-44761

Printed in the United States of America.

10 9 8 7 6 5 4 3 2

For Patrick and Suzanne,
without whom none of this would have ever happened

About the Author

Patrick H. Sullivan, DBA, MS, BS is an acknowledged expert at extracting profits from intellectual assets. He has emerged as a key conceptual thinker in the field of value extraction, having already published two books on the topic. He is a founding partner of the ICM Group, LLC, a consulting company providing advice and services in the extraction of value from intellectual capital. His consulting practice involves assessing the value extraction capabilities and needs of corporations, developing IC strategies that enable and enhance corporate business strategies, assessing the IC management needs of corporations, and designing and implementing decision processes and management systems for extracting value.

Dr. Sullivan is a frequent speaker, giving talks on a range of intellectual capital management issues, including strategy, IC and corporate value, licensing, and developing profits from IC. He is a regular contributor of articles to *Les Nouvelles,* the journal of the Licensing Executives Society as well as a sought-after contributor of papers and chapters to anthologies on intellectual capital or intellectual property. He is a Fellow of the American Council on Education, and a member of the American Bar Association Intellectual Property Section, the Licensing Executives Society (where he is the founding chairman of the Intellectual

Capital Management Committee). He is included in Who's Who and Who's Who in California.

An engineering graduate of the U.S. Naval Academy, Dr. Sullivan has been a naval gunnery officer and an engineer on the launch team of the Apollo/Saturn project at Cape Kennedy. Following graduate studies in business, he was chief financial officer at two research universities. He has been a Principal Consultant at SRI International, where he managed the firm's general consulting practice in Europe, and a Vice President of the MAC Group consultancy.

In addition to consulting, writing, and speaking, Dr. Sullivan testifies as a court approved expert in matters involving intellectual property valuation and damages. In addition to his undergraduate degree in General Engineering, he holds a masters degree in R&D Management and a doctorate in Business Administration.

Foreword

We are living in a New Economy—an economy characterized by new technologies, globalization, and an ever increasing emphasis on intangibles. New technologies are creating new transactions and new markets, and giving rise to new opportunities and new risks. The Internet is accelerating the globalization trend, as knowledge is created and exchanged and business more easily transacted across borders. The focus of this New Economy is on knowledge and relationships, with a premium awarded to firms demonstrating a capability for speed, flexibility, innovation, and the ability to connect.

Arthur Andersen's view is that intangible assets will be increasingly important to creating value in the New Economy, while the traditional physical assets of the industrial age will continue their decline in relative importance. Indeed, many of the most successful companies in the New Economy will be built on the power of intellectual capital and on their application of information technologies. At the same time, the capital markets are recognizing fundamentally new ways of creating value. More and more, the successful companies will be those knowing how to make the best use of employee knowledge, processes, relationships, and a host of other nontraditional assets.

Arthur Andersen is involved in several areas of research to learn more about how firms can be successful in this New Economy. We believe that the management of intellectual capital will be one of the cornerstone capabilities in the New Economy. We wish to encourage thought leaders around the world to contribute to the business community's knowledge and understanding of how to create and extract more value from these key intangible assets. With this in mind, we are proud to sponsor this new series of books in cooperation with John Wiley & Sons, Inc., on the topic of intellectual capital and its management.

This first book in the series, authored by Patrick H. Sullivan, makes a significant and timely contribution to the body of knowledge about how businesses create and extract value through intellectual capital. It offers insights into the major components of intellectual capital—intellectual assets and intellectual property. And it provides key insights about the importance of intellectual capital to various industries and types of organizations. The goal of this book can be summed up simply: to explain how to extract the most value from your intellectual capital! Success for many organizations in the New Economy will depend on how they use all of their intellectual assets to create value.

We are pleased to be a part of the new thinking on the management of intangibles and we hope that this book, and those that will follow in this series, will advance our collective understanding of this increasingly important area of management.

Jim Wadia
Worldwide Managing Partner
Arthur Andersen

Preface

Every so often we find, with hindsight, that we did something in life that was either very wise or very lucky. In 1995, I did both. I was one of the founders of an informal group comprised of company executives whose jobs involved converting intellectual capital into profits. This group, ultimately calling itself the ICM Gathering (for intellectual capital managers), has added value to each of its members. Speaking only for myself, it has provided me with some of the most intellectually exciting experiences possible and has done so continually for five years.

The Gathering companies meet three times each year to share individual experiences and to learn about extracting value from intangible assets. With each succeeding meeting, filled as they have been with companies discussing their successes and failures, we taught each other more and more about techniques, methods, and processes. As time went on, I found myself trying to put together a collective "so what." I sensed that there was some sort of pattern or overarching model that might emerge from the collection of individual company learnings. This search for collective learnings led me to what would become a self-appointed role as the person responsible for pulling together generic models from all of the Gathering conversations, meetings, and discussions.

In mid-1995, my partners and I founded the ICM Group, a consulting company focused on advising clients on the extraction of value from their intellectual assets. My partners quickly became equally as excited as I with the Gathering and soon immersed themselves into the teaching and sharing of information with other member companies as well as helping with the convening and hosting of meetings.

By 1997, the Gathering had decided that each member company would benefit if more corporations became involved in managing their intellectual assets and shared what they had learned. This thinking led the ICM Gathering to the writing and publication of *Profiting from Intellectual Capital: Extracting Value from Innovation*, in 1998. I played my self-appointed role, pulling together the collective learnings, while individual companies wrote about how they applied what they had learned to their own company through the Gathering. *Profiting* was the first attempt at putting onto paper the lessons of a group of companies who successfully extracted value from their hidden assets and moved it to the company's bottom line. Looking back, however, *Profiting* is perhaps more difficult to read and the lessons not as easily extractable as we would have liked. Likewise, *Profiting* was published by John Wiley & Sons, Inc., as part of their intellectual property series and was narrowly marketed to professionals in the fields of IP law and licensing.

As 1999 came along, I found myself wanting to do several things with my next generation of learning from the ICM Gathering. First, I wanted a book on value extraction that was available to everyone, not just technical professionals. Second, I wanted a book that was easier and more helpful to read than *Profiting*. Third, I wanted to put into calculable terms what I had learned about converting intangible assets into value. And finally, I wanted to make it clear that managing intellectual capital involved more than knowledge management or computers or information systems; that fundamentally it was about *value,* how to create it and how then to extract it for the benefit of the organization.

This book is written to accomplish the above four objectives. Let me know how well I accomplished each of them.

Patrick H. Sullivan
Palo Alto, California

Acknowledgments

Books are funny things. The thoughts they contain don't spring full-blown from the author's brain but rather emerge in fits and starts from conversations with others, and from contemplation of the ideas, accomplishments, and writings of others. One of my favorite stories on this topic concerns Albert Einstein. Someone, as the story goes, was complimenting the great man about the clarity, creativity, and insight he brought to the field of physics when he published his work on the theory of relativity. Einstein is reported to have responded to these kind thoughts by remarking that if indeed he had provided the universe with a new view of itself, he had only "stood on the shoulders of giants." Einstein meant, of course, that from his perspective all that he had done was to weave together and perhaps slightly expand upon the excellent work done earlier by other thinkers in his field.

In my case, the others are colleagues, acquaintances, friends, and partners. Their individual perspectives, insights, projects, and creative activities have provided me with the rich array of ideas that underlie virtually all of what is found in this book. In particular the members of the ICM Gathering have been instrumental in thinking through, applying, modifying, and improving the techniques and methods of intellectual capital management. The shared learning from the past two years of discussions and experiences of the ICM Gathering companies have been stimulating, exciting, provocative, and incredibly valuable to me in the development of my own thinking as well as in providing the concepts and methods for this book.

For the past year my firm and I have been working closely with Arthur Andersen, LLP, in a strategic alliance focused on expanding the availability of intellectual property management services to the widest range of interested companies. As part of our alliance, we are tapping into each other's intellectual capital to jointly develop ways of leveraging intellectual property for the benefit of our clients. Although this joint development activity is just beginning, it offers great promise for new and exciting ideas. In the course of my work with Andersen, I have been enriched by the ideas of Julie Davis, Peter King, Richard Boulton, Barry Lippert, Ed Ginault, and Lorraine Morrison. I would specifically like to thank Julie for her ideas on a hierarchy of value; Peter for his contributions on differentiable assets; and Richard, Barry, and Ed for their perspective on asset allocation and intellectual capital.

I would like to mention Aurigin Systems, Inc., a software firm specializing in software for managing intellectual assets from a business perspective. Three people from this firm have been particularly helpful to me in the development of concepts and the translation of those thoughts into practical methods and practices. First and foremost is Kevin Rivette, the CEO of Aurigin. Kevin has been helpful on several fronts, not the least of which is providing encouragement at every step of the conceptualization process. Second, I would like to acknowledge Dan'l Lewin, President of Aurigin, for his critical eye and his intellectual honesty in continually pressing to know more about how an interesting conceptual enterprise was practical and how it could produce the cash which businesses so fundamentally need. And finally, I would like to acknowledge Paul Germeraad, formerly the VP of research for Avery-Dennison (and member of the ICM Gathering) and now Vice President of Aurigin systems. Paul has been a particularly creative thinker in the realm of value extraction. His insights and abilities to express complex thoughts and concepts through the use of graphics and symbols taught me much about a capability that is increasingly important to people involved in intellectual capital management.

Professional friends and colleagues have been another source of inspiration for the ideas contained between these covers. In particular I have been influenced by Karl-Erik Sveiby whose ideas and whose book on human capital, its measurement, and its management are among the most advanced and insightful I have seen. In the same field, my friend and colleague Hubert St. Onge continues to be the source of innovative ideas, new perspectives, and precepts that guide how we think about and manage our firms' human assets. Several other pioneers in the field of intellectual capital management should also be mentioned for the impact their work had on this book's contents: Gordon Petrash of PricewaterhouseCoopers (formerly of Dow Chemical) for his work in systematizing value extraction; Leif Edvinsson, of Skandia, for his contributions in publicizing the idea of intellectual capital; Tom Stewart of *Fortune* magazine for his pioneering articles on brainpower and intellectual capital; David Teece of the University of California Berkeley for his seminal economic work in extracting value from innovation; Paul Adler of the University of Southern California for his contributions to improving and expanding upon the early conceptual underpinnings of value extraction; Baruch Lev of New York University's Stern School of Business for his analytical frameworks and studies that have dispelled many of the myths surrounding the effect that intellectual assets may have on the corporation and on its value; and Ron Kasznik of Stanford who had the good sense and good fortune to marry Efrat, from whom I have learned more about accounting as an analytical tool than from anyone else I know.

Martha Cooley, my friend and editor at John Wiley & Sons, was my co-conspirator in the early thinking of this book. As it neared completion, Martha's suggestions and pointed criticisms vastly improved what would otherwise have been a much more pedestrian effort.

Many authors close their acknowledgments with thanks to their wives and children for their forbearance and patience during the awful "writing time." A bachelor, I live alone except for a sweet, but petulant cat whose only noticeable reaction to my "writing time" has been mild unhappiness should feeding times ever have been delayed.

But of greatest importance for acknowledgment are my business partners, close friends, and, coincidentally, my children, Suzanne Harrison and Patrick Sullivan, Jr., to whom I am most grateful. Without their thoughts, encouragement, and willingness to shoulder my load when circumstances demanded, the enterprise of the ICM Group, this book, or indeed my own efforts at learning, consulting, and writing would have been ever so much less fruitful. I want to acknowledge them for their academic and business achievements, each of them having carved out an enviable personal and professional reputation within the field of ICM. Further, I would like to openly confess that without their assistance, support, and ideas this book would never have been possible.

Contents

Part III   Managing Intellectual Capital

8   EXTRACTING VALUE FROM INTELLECTUAL PROPERTY   127

9   EXTRACTING VALUE FROM INTELLECTUAL ASSETS   155

10   EXTRACTING VALUE FROM HUMAN CAPITAL (BASIC CONCEPTS)   173

Value-Driven
Intellectual Capital

Part I

The Relationship Between Intellectual Capital and Corporate Value

1

Introduction

Intellectual capital exploded onto the business scene in the 1990s. When *Fortune* magazine published Tom Stewart's article "Brainpower," in 1991, it was the first article on the topic to appear in a national business magazine. By 1998, a number of books and dozens of articles in professional journals and trade magazines were devoted to the topic, to say nothing of significant coverage in the popular business magazines such as *Fortune* and *Forbes*. In 1999 alone, over a dozen conferences were held around the world on intellectual capital management in one form or another.

In 1999, *CEO Magazine* and Arthur Andersen hosted a roundtable luncheon for chief executive officers (CEOs) interested in discussing intellectual capital (IC) and its impact on the firm as we know it. The luncheon drew 17 CEOs representing both manufacturing and service industry companies. All were intrigued by the potential hidden value that the intellectual capital perspective suggests lies untapped within their businesses, but none knew what kinds of value they could obtain from their company's intangible assets or how they might go about it. They just knew that there was hidden value in their companies and that it was somehow wrapped up in the thoughts, skills, innovations, and abilities of their employees. They wanted to learn more about this value: how to harness it, direct it, and extract value from it.

This book is written for those CEOs and for anyone else who wants to know how to extract the hidden value that resides within the firm's intellectual capital. As of this writing dozens of firms actively engage in extracting value from their IC. The people directing the activities for these firms have formed a community (called the ICM Gathering) to share their ideas and success stories. With the exception of a very few proprietary bits of information that could be useful to competitors, these firms are willing to share their knowledge, and this book draws heavily on their experiences. The purpose of this book is to help businesses profit from one of their most important assets, their intellectual capital.

WHAT IS INTELLECTUAL CAPITAL?

The idea of capital as a euphemism for a strategic business asset is not new. Economists frequently describe the basic resources necessary for an industrial enterprise in terms of the three classic kinds of assets: land, labor, and capital (here capital refers to financial and other economic assets). But the idea of intellectual capital is a new one; it brings to the foreground the brainpower assets of the organization, recognizing them as having a degree of importance comparable to the traditional land, labor, and tangible assets.

If a survey were conducted, there would be agreement that many modern companies are filled with intellectual capital: law firms, consulting firms, software companies, computer companies to name but a few. But if the survey went on to ask people to define what intellectual capital is, there would be a wide range of answers. These answers would not converge onto one simple definition of intellectual capital, but rather on many. The range of views and the number of terms used to describe and define intellectual capital are broad, without a clear focus, and often confusing. Some of the same terms appear in many of the definitions yet seem to have different meanings in each.

For example, the following list of "capitals" is frequently, and differently, used in descriptions or definitions of intellectual capital: human capital, customer capital, stakeholder capital, cultural capital, relationship capital, organizational capital, structural capital, process capital, and economic capital.

In contrast to the list of confusing and ever-changing *types* of capital, there is substantial agreement on the activities and elements that constitute the capital of interest here: intellectual capital. Picture the elements of IC as balloons in a pile. They might look like Exhibit 1.1. If the balloons were piled on the floor of a room, each observer in a different part of the room would have a different perspective on intellectual capital. Someone interested in knowledge or knowledge management would see one face of the pile. From another perspective, the elements of intellectual capital would present a different face.

The diversity of opinion on just exactly what intellectual capital is results from the wide range of interests and perspectives on the subject. Each definition is consistent with the perspective and interests of its users and understandably often neglects or ignores the interests or perspectives of others. The users of intellectual capital tend to fall into several groups as

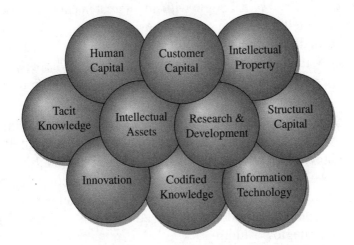

Exhibit 1.1   Elements Comprising Intellectual Capital

listed below, each with strongly held and sometimes vehemently defended points of view.

- *Knowledge and learning.* People with these interests tend to see human capital and the tacit components of intellectual capital in the foreground. They are concerned primarily with the creation of new or more knowledge and methods and environments in which creative processes can be most productive.

- *Knowledge management.* This term is often used as a synonym for computer-based information systems. People with this area of interest concern themselves with the identification of data or information, where it resides, where it needs to be, and how to get it from point A to point B in the most efficient manner.

- *Innovation management.* This term is sometimes used to describe the management of research and development (R&D). People with this interest focus on how to improve the efficiency and effectiveness with which ideas are generated and screened to identify those of greatest interest or value to the organization.

- *Capital markets.* People with an interest in capital markets see intellectual capital as a business asset and are concerned with the *amount* of a firm's intellectual capital, how it is valued, how its value affects the company balance sheet, and how to provide value information to current and potential stockholders.

- *Shareholders.* People in this group have a financial interest in a business enterprise. They see the firm's intellectual capital as a business asset and are interested in both the amount and the use of a firm's intellectual capital. Their interest usually centers on how the intellectual capital can be focused and leveraged to improve profitability or strategic positioning.

- *Company managers.* These are the people who manage the firm's intellectual capital. They, too, see it as a business asset, but their focus is on how to manage it in order to increase both its amount and, more important, its ability to increase cash flow. Company managers involved with intellectual capital are most often focused on creating the firm's *future* cash flow, economic profit, and sustainable competitive advantage.

Exhibit 1.2 illustrates how the view of IC from different perspectives results in different elements appearing in the foreground and background of each view.

HOW DOES IC BRING VALUE TO A FIRM?

Once a firm understands that it has intellectual capital, how does it convert it into something of value? The answer is that *it*

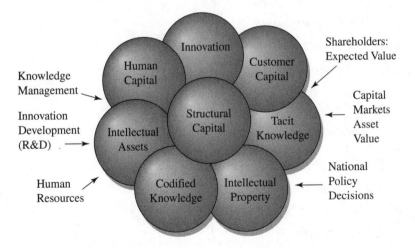

Exhibit 1.2   Different Perspectives on Intellectual Capital

depends! For example, to a company's chief financial officer something is valuable to the extent that it has a positive effect on the firm's financial statement. CFOs tend to ask how much revenue or profit this "IC stuff" generates on a sustained basis. In contrast, a marketing executive may find the strategic positioning made possible by the firm's IC to be valuable. At a recent meeting of the ICM Gathering, member companies, all sophisticated in extracting value from their intellectual capital, were asked to describe how their firms had received value from their intellectual assets. The list that follows shows their response.

Profit Generation
Income from products or services, through:
  sale
  licensing royalties
  joint venture income
  strategic alliance income
Income from patents, through:
  sale
  licensing royalties
  joint venture income
  donation (tax write-off)
Price premiums
Increase in sales, through:
  convoyed sales

Strategic Positioning
Market share
Leadership (innovation, technology, etc.)
Standard-setting
Name recognition, through:

branding

trademarking

reputation

Acquiring innovations of others

Customer loyalty

Cost reductions

Improved productivity

Repeat sales

Long-term sales

On average, each of these companies was receiving four or five kinds of value from its intellectual capital. The value many of these firms receive from their IC is the result of a well-reasoned, well-planned, and well-executed set of management initiatives designed to ensure that specific forms of value deemed important to the business strategy are routinely extracted from the firm's intellectual capital.

STRATEGY AND ITS EFFECT ON VALUE

Different kinds of firms use different strategies to obtain different mixes of value from their intellectual capital. Firms that sell physical products often protect their product innovations by patenting them. The profits of these firms derive from the sale of differentiable products. In other words, they seek innovations from their human capital that will make the company's products different from those of their competitors and attractive to customers. Such firms are likely to seek value from their IC in the form of income from product sales. They may also be expected to seek value in the form of strategic positioning, specifically by creating a reputation or image and using it to generate customer loyalty.

Other kinds of firms profit by selling the knowledge of their human capital. Consulting firms, accounting firms, and law firms are examples. The value these firms can expect to obtain from their intellectual capital is in the fees they receive for services provided to their clients. In addition to income for services provided, these firms may also seek value in the form of reputation or image. The fundamental nature and functions of a firm may be a primary determinant of its strategy and the kind of value it can and should extract from its intellectual capital. The point can be illustrated by a description of four different kinds of firms.

1. *Differentiated products company.* This type of company earns its profits from the sale of differentiable products. Companies in this category sell products in a retail environment. Hewlett-Packard is a good example of this kind of company because its profits derive from product sales and its IC focuses on product innovations that allow it to charge a premium price.

2. *Commodity products company.* This type of company earns its profits from the sale of commodity products, for example bulk chemical manufacturers. Such firms sell tonnage of commodity chemicals to long-term customers. Its innovations tend to focus on reducing manufacturing costs.

3. *A network services company.* This type of firm uses technology to create a network over which customers communicate with one another (i.e., telecommunications/wireless services company). The network becomes the distribution channel through which the firm markets its products and services. Profits are derived from customer "network time or use." The business is driven by market share, which itself is strongly affected by the "quality" of the network and the attractiveness of products and services offered. Innovation focuses on creating, improving, and maintaining network quality and on creating and im-

proving products and services. Telephone and utilities companies are good examples of this kind of company.

4. *A direct services company.* This kind of service company charges an hourly fee for providing its services. Law firms, consulting firms, and accounting firms are examples of direct services companies.

Exhibit 1.3 shows what kinds of value each kind of company would be likely to seek from its intellectual capital. The product firms seek value through product income across the spectrum of income-producing mechanisms. Services firms seek income predominantly through a narrow spectrum of mechanisms.

While all firms seek strategic positioning value, there is significant variability in the amount and kind of strategic positioning value desired. Differences in company type and/or strategy may lead to significant differences in the kind of value a firm expects to realize through its IC. Some kinds of firms (a telecommunications firm, for example) seek a significant portion of the value from their IC in the form of strategic position, image, reputation, market share, etc. Other firms seek to realize value in the form of income or revenue. Still others seek IC value in the form of strategic position or a mixture of income and strategic position. Each firm must develop an appropriate strategy for realizing the value(s) it seeks from its IC. How should it define and measure these values? What activities does it need to undertake to produce these values? How does a firm ensure that the value it wishes to extract from IC is appropriate for its business strategy?

How can a company manage the extraction of value from both intellectual property and intellectual assets? How does anyone value firms, such as these where a significant portion of the firm's value is associated with its intangible intellectual capital?

This book attempts to answer these questions and others that follow from them.

	Differentiated Products	Commodity Products	Network Services	Direct Services
Profit Generation				
Product or Svc.				
Sale	X	X	X	X
License		X		
Joint Venture	X	X		
Stgc. Alliance	X	X		
IP Income				
Sale	X	X	X	
Lic. Royalties		X	X	
Joint Venture	X	X	X	
Donation	X	X	X	
Price Premium	X		X	X
Increase in Sales				
Convoyed	X			X
Repeat	X			X
Long-Term	X			
Cost Reduction	X			
Productivity Imp.	X			
Strategic Position				
Market Share	X		X	
Leadership	X		X	X
Standard Setting	X		X	X
Name Recog.	X		X	X
Branding	X		X	X
Trademarking	X	X	X	X
Reputation	X	X	X	X
Cust. Loyalty	X	X	X	X

Exhibit 1.3   A Matrix of Different Value Sought from IC by Different Kinds of Firms

A BRIEF HISTORY

As mentioned earlier, the subject of intellectual capital appeared on the business scene in the 1990s, as if shot from a cannon. By the end of the decade, the term intellectual capital had been transformed from an interesting new idea to a frequently used and well-understood phrase in the business lexicon.

However, this history actually began in the early 1980s, as managers, academics, and consultants around the world began to notice that a firm's intangible assets, its intellectual capital, were often a major determinant of the corporation's profits. For example, in Japan, circa 1980, Hiroyuki Itami noticed the difference in performance among Japanese companies, and after some study attributed it to differences in the firms' intangible assets. His published analysis concluded that intangible assets are "unattainable with money alone, are capable of multiple, simultaneous use, and yield multiple, simultaneous benefits."[1] In 1986, Karl-Erik Sveiby, the manager and owner of a Sweden-based publishing company, published *The Knowledge Company*—a book, written in Swedish, that explained how to manage these intangible assets. It was the first book in the world to deal with this subject and inspired the very early "Swedish Movement" in knowledge management and intellectual capital in both research and practice. Sveiby, today a Professor at Macquarie Graduate School of Management, and a leading thinker in the field, noted that:

Managers in some of the fastest-growing and most profitable businesses focus on knowledge, see their businesses from a knowledge perspective, and act as if their intangible assets are real assets. By freeing themselves from the mental straitjackets of the industrial age, some of these pioneer managers have found, seemingly by accident sometimes, a wellspring of limitless resources arising from the infinite human ability to create knowledge and

13

from the convenient fact that, unlike conventional assets, knowledge grows when it is shared.[2]

During the 1980s the prevalent view of business strategy was based on the "competitive forces" perspective pioneered by Michael Porter of Harvard University. This approach views strategy formulation as relating to a company and its competitive environment. According to this view, competitive advantage lies with the ability to find "holes" in the market and then to fill those holes with products and services while defending one's market position against all possible competitors. During the course of the 1980s others were formulating an alternative view; some American economists developed the view of business strategy based on the resources of the firm and the efficiency with which they are used. This resource-based view of business strategy postulates that firms can create strategic advantage over their competitors by developing unique combinations of tangible and intellectual resources and capabilities.

The resource-based perspective notes that firms are not homogeneous, that they have very distinct individual characteristics and resources, such as unique buildings, facilities, people, and ideas. Further, each firm's resources are "sticky," at least in the short run. That is, firms are to some degree stuck with what they have and may have to live with what they lack. The stickiness arises for two reasons. First, business development is an extremely complex process. Firms lack the organizational capacity to develop new competencies quickly. Second, some assets are simply not readily obtainable on the open market, for example, tacit know-how. Firms with superior systems and structures (i.e., resources) are profitable to the degree that they can develop advantages such as markedly lower costs or markedly higher quality or product performance. Whereas the competitive forces strategy operates "downstream" of the resource allocation and internal operations of the firm, the resources-based strategy derives competitive advantage "upstream" of product markets. It rests on the firm's idiosyncratic and difficult-to-imitate resources and their use.

In 1986, University of California Berkeley business school professor David Teece wrote "Profiting from Technological Innovation," an article that pulled together much of the then-current thinking of members of the resources-based strategy school. He identified a series of steps necessary for the extraction of value from innovation. The explication of these steps meant that for the first time managers could learn, and subsequently teach their staffs, how to maximize the value of their firms' innovations.

In 1991 and 1992, Tom Stewart, a staff writer at *Fortune* magazine, wrote two articles on "brainpower" in which he discussed the idea that the company's intellectual capital—in other words, its employees—had much to do with its profitability or success. Also in 1991, Skandia AFS organized the first corporate intellectual capital office and named Leif Edvinsson as its Vice President for Intellectual Capital. Edvinsson's mission was to learn how others were managing intellectual capital and using it to generate profits.

In 1993, The Dow Chemical Company, interested in developing new profits from its intellectual capital, began trying to identify ideas or innovations that might have been previously overlooked and to select and develop those ideas with the greatest profit-making potential. Dow named Gordon Petrash as its first Director of Intellectual Assets.

After reading David Teece's article, I became fascinated with the idea that there could be a systematic set of decisions and rules that companies could use to extract profits from their innovations. I refined and expanded on Teece's ideas with a view toward developing a consulting service focused on developing profits from innovation. Teece and I collaborated on our first consulting project in this area in 1990, giving a set of day-long seminars to DuPont executives. I continued to develop the profiting theme. In 1993, I met Gordon Petrash and Leif

Edvinsson and we eventually created an informal network of companies that were actively developing profits from their intellectual capital. This was the genesis of the ICM Gathering.

By the mid 1990s it was becoming clear that there were two separate but related paths of thinking about intellectual capital. One path, the knowledge and brainpower path, focused on creating and expanding the firm's knowledge (as espoused by Stewart, Edvinsson, Sveiby, and others). The other path, the resource-based perspective, was concerned with how to create profits from a firm's unique combinations of intellectual and tangible resources (Itami, Teece, Sullivan, and others).

THE ICM GATHERING

Companies interested in profiting from the intellectual assets they already owned spurred the evolution of intellectual capital management. In Skandia's case, intellectual capital included both its employees and its network of insurance brokers. In Dow's case, intellectual capital comprised the ideas and innovations stuffed into the file drawers and folders of its scientists and engineers. Intellectual capital management became the vehicle by which companies came to learn more about their intellectual capital. By 1994 there were perhaps a dozen companies around the world engaged in the active extraction of profits from their intellectual capital.

Petrash, Edvinsson, and I agreed that it would be highly interesting and instructive to convene a meeting of representatives of all of the companies who were actively extracting value from their intangible assets. This would allow us to get each company's perspective on both intellectual capital (i.e., what it is) and how to profit from it (i.e., how to manage it). We gathered eight of the twelve companies together in January 1995 (Dow, DuPont, Hoffman LaRoche, Skandia, Hewlett-Packard, Hughes Space Systems, and the Law and Economics Consulting Group). At the end of an opening round of show-and-tell it was clear that each company saw intellectual capital differently and managed its resources in this area differently as well. Through subsequent discussion we came to understand that while using the same terms, each company defined them differently. We proceeded to develop a common set of definitions and descriptions. Using this newly agreed-upon set of terms, we learned that although we each approached intellectual capital differently, we were all dealing with the same thing.

The company representatives involved in this meeting felt as if they had found long-lost relatives. Each had been operating in a vacuum without knowing there were others also trying to deal with the same problems. The group decided to meet again. In 1999, a group of thirty companies met three times a year as the ICM Gathering.

At its first meeting, the ICM Gathering determined that it needed to agree on a definition of the term "intellectual capital," as well as an understanding of its major elements. In pursuing that goal, the members first created a definition of IC that was consistent with their collective responsibilities to their companies. Because the participants in the Gathering held positions such as chief IP counsel, director of intellectual asset management, laboratory director (with financial responsibility), and licensing director, they were more focused on the creation of profits than the creation of knowledge. Thus it is not surprising that the Gathering defined intellectual capital as "knowledge that can be converted into profits."

A graphical representation of intellectual capital was created to depict the components of IC and their relationships to one another. This graphic, shown in Exhibit 1.4, shows the major elements of intellectual capital: humans (with their embedded tacit knowledge) and codified knowledge. Codified knowledge has come to be called the firm's "intellectual assets" (IA). When someone's tacit knowledge is committed to paper (it could also be canvas, electronic media, or any other medium), it becomes a codified asset of the firm. Some of these codified assets (called "intellectual assets") are legally protected as

Intellectual Capital

Human Capital	Intellectual Assets	
Experience	Programs	Methodologies
	Inventions	Documents
Know-how	Processes	Drawings
	Databases	Designs
Skills		
Creativity	**Intellectual Property**	
	Patents	
	Copyright	
	Trademarks	
	Trade Secrets	

Exhibit 1.4   Intellectual Capital and Its Major Components

patents, copyrights, trademarks, trade secrets, or semiconductor masks. Intellectual assets that are legally protected are referred to by the legal term "intellectual property."

OVERVIEW OF THE BOOK

This book is about the value intellectual capital brings to an organization as well as how to determine the specific kind of value desired; how to organize the firm in order to systematically obtain the desired value; and how to measure the value realized (whether in terms of its impact on company value (stock price) or company strategic position). The intellectual capital management portions of the book relate to all knowledge companies, although many of the examples relate to technology-based companies, the kinds of companies comprising the ICM Gathering.

This first chapter has highlighted many of the key ideas discussed in later chapters. The reader interested in knowing the "map" of what is contained in the book, and where specific information is located, should find the following outline helpful.

The book is comprised of three major parts:

- Part I The Relationship Between Intellectual Capital and Corporate Value (Chapters 1–4)
- Part II Valuing Knowledge Companies (Chapters 5–7)
- Part III Managing Intellectual Capital (Chapters 8–12)

Part I The Relationship Between Intellectual Capital and Corporate Value

Chapter 1 opens with a discussion of intellectual capital and its importance to the audiences to be addressed. The chapter outlines some of the basic concepts underlying corporate value: quantitative value (in the form of cash flow (current and future)); and qualitative value (strategic position and others).

Chapter 2 discusses what a framework is and how it is useful to managers. The chapter outlines the four key elements of the IC framework: the definition of intellectual capital, an economic model of an IC company, the linkage between strategy, IC, and profits; and a model of a system for managing the firm's IC.

Chapter 3 discusses the kinds of value that intellectual capital provides to the firm. These include direct and indirect, offensive and defensive, and internal and external value. Although these different kinds of value have now been made explicit, the link between the basic innovation that is the source of the value and the realization of that value has not yet been defined. Two further questions remain: How does a firm identify the activities within the firm that make the IC value appear? How does a firm manage and measure progress toward achieving the anticipated value?

Chapter 4 deals with the ways managers may determine which activities are required to produce the firm's anticipated IC value. It is also concerned with how managers may better focus their activities and resources. In cases where there are two, three, or more kinds of IC value anticipated, and all may not require the same set of activities to produce the value, the chapter discusses how managers can prioritize their resource allocation decisions.

Part II Valuing Knowledge Companies

Chapter 5 discusses the different reasons for valuing a knowledge company and for each of these reasons, the methods and approaches that are the most useful. The chapter also discusses why the accounting framework is not useful for valuing intangibles and why a different approach to valuation is more appropriate in the case of intellectual capital.

Chapter 6 identifies a series of steps for companies wishing to implement an ICM capability for managing their intellectual capital. While the chapter is focused on the issues facing technology companies, much of what is included relates to all knowledge companies, not just those commercializing technology. The areas of greatest importance are highlighted as defining the firm's vision and long-term strategy, describing the context within which the firm operates, defining the role(s) for intellectual capital, designing the intellectual property and intellectual asset management systems, and describing and implementing the IC management capability desired by the firm. The steps outlined in this chapter are gleaned from the experiences of all of the firms in the ICM Gathering.

Chapter 7 addresses the following questions: When determining how much to pay for a knowledge company being acquired, how does the potential purchaser make the calculation? Is the frame of reference an accounting or financial one? Or is it an intellectual capital one? Too often, companies being acquired are valued based on old-fashioned or no-longer-applicable methods. This chapter discusses some new ideas about how to value knowledge companies for acquisition or merger.

Part III Managing Intellectual Capital

Chapter 8 covers extracting value from intellectual property. Intellectual property management is a key set of concepts, methods, and processes designed for aligning the intellectual properties of the firm with its business strategies and objectives. A firm that wants to maximize the value extracted from its portfolio of intellectual properties must have several key elements in place. This chapter describes the key elements involved in extracting value from intellectual property, including key decisions and decision-making processes, including who is involved, what information is needed by the decision-makers, what work processes are necessary to provide this information, what databases are needed to store the information, and how each decision will be implemented.

Chapter 9 discusses the similarities and the differences between IP and IA and the implications this has for the IC management process. Extracting value from intellectual assets, the company's codified knowledge, builds upon the system for extracting value from intellectual property. Intellectual asset management (IAM) is similar to intellectual property management (IPM) in that it uses the same conceptual basis that specifies innovation and complementary assets as the primary sources of value for the firm.

Chapter 10 describes the relationship between knowledge, knowledge types, and intellectual capital. It introduces the relationship between knowledge and profits, the concept of value creation and value extraction, and shows how a firm can determine whether the two sets of activities are in balance.

Chapter 11 contains several key management concepts relating to the firm's human capital, from the perspective of someone interested in extracting value. These include the concept of core human capital as well a discussion of the two areas of focus for core human capital: creativity and productivity.

Chapter 12 lays out a step-by-step approach for how companies can create an in-house capability for managing their intellectual capital, building on the information in the preceding chapters and the knowledge of the companies in the ICM Gathering. Using the information in this chapter, firms can improve, start up, or modify their own capability for extracting value from innovation.

Appendix

The basic language, terms, and definitions used in the text are described in the appendix. It also includes a discussion of the Value Extraction models for intellectual capital and for knowledge companies. It describes some of the basic concepts underlying vision, strategy, value, and valuation. The appendix also discusses principles underlying value creation and value extraction, including concepts and general strategies as well as the approaches used by specific companies. It identifies the sources of value for knowledge companies and discusses the mechanisms used to convert value into cash. It reviews the decision to commercialize, in which companies determine the number and kind of mechanisms they will use to develop cash from their innovations.

NOTES

1. Itami, pp. 12,13.
2. Sveiby, p. x.

2

A Framework for Intellectual Capital Management

We have already defined knowledge companies as those that derive profits from their intellectual capital. For most people, this definition brings to mind Microsoft, Xerox, or IBM, companies that have a reputation for bringing new ideas and innovations to market. While these companies fit an ideal image of the knowledge company, many more companies fit the description as well. Indeed, from an intellectual capital perspective all companies are knowledge companies. How could they not be? Is there a business that does not involve some bit of innovation or knowledge in its enterprise?

The reason most of us do not see all companies as knowledge companies is that we are used to looking at them from a business perspective, not an intellectual capital perspective. The CEO of a forest products company once lamented to me about the lack of intellectual capital in his industry. He defined intellectual capital as some form of sophisticated technology. In an effort to impress me with his company's attempts to fill this IC void, he told me that his firm had recently purchased and installed some sophisticated computer-controlled machinery for milling logs but that it had been unable to produce the same amount of usable lumber per log as the company's human sawmill operators. When I pointed out to him that the mill hands and their knowledge and know-how were the very essence of intellectual capital for his firm, he looked surprised and then acknowledged that he had never considered intellectual capital in that way.

The point of this story is that the CEO did not really understand what intellectual capital is. He did not look at his company as one containing unique knowledge and skills or a unique set of business assets that differentiate it from its competitors. Getting such a perspective requires nothing more than applying some definitions and models to the aspects of the firm one wishes to examine. Here we want to look at the firm to find its hidden value, the value it can exploit to make it unique in the marketplace. In particular, we are interested in the uniqueness contributed by the firm's intellectual capital.

Unfortunately we see companies largely in two dimensions, the first being the physical dimension, which involves seeing the company very much as a photographer would. Imagine looking at a company scrapbook or photo album. You might see pictures of the corporate office building, the manufacturing facilities, groups of employees smiling up at the camera, stacks of raw materials, as well as finished product sitting on the loading dock. This is the physical view we all have of our companies.

The second dimension through which we view companies is the accounting dimension. Here we see the firm's tangible assets listed on the balance sheet along with the firm's outstanding liabilities. We see income and expenditures associated with its operations carefully listed on the profit and loss statement, with the dollar amounts of expenditures for goods or activities carefully recorded.

Sadly for knowledge companies, neither of the two standard

dimensions makes it possible for us to see the firm's intellectual capital (its knowledge that can be converted into profit). This chapter is about creating the set of polarized glasses to allow the hidden assets of the firm to become visible. We will discuss the framework as well as provide a different way of looking at the firm's tangible assets, one that shows the attributes of these assets that contribute to the firm's ability to convert its hidden value into profits.

As you read this chapter, try to change the way you view your own company. Try to redefine it in intellectual capital terms. Think of the company's vision and strategy in ways that allow you to define one or more roles for intellectual capital. Think of your company's assets, not in terms of their appearance on its balance sheet, but in terms of their degree of intangibility. The degree to which you can redefine your company into IC terms is the degree to which the concepts in this book will be valuable to you.

THE IC FRAMEWORK

Managing the activities related to intellectual capital can be a daunting and confusing task, in part because the field of ICM is young and there does not yet exist a well-articulated and easy-to-understand structure or framework that helps to put the bits and pieces of intellectual capital information into an orderly perspective.

The following framework is one that the participant companies in the ICM Gathering have developed and find useful. The framework has three major dimensions (see Exhibit 2.1). The first involves the firm's context: its vision strategy and the roles it has assigned to its intellectual capital. The second involves a way of redefining the firm in non-accounting terms, and the third involves the activities associated with actively managing the firm's intangible assets.

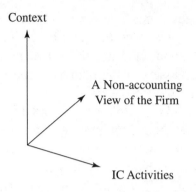

Context

A Non-accounting
View of the Firm

IC Activities

Exhibit 2.1   Three Dimensions of the IC Framework

THE FIRST DIMENSION: CONTEXT

All firms operate within the context of a long-term vision and business strategy. These provide direction and guidance for the decisions made routinely by the people operating the intellectual asset management system (IAMS). Firms that have learned to create value from their intellectual assets have learned how to link their IAMS with their vision and strategy.

Vision

Making the linkage involves an *a priori* review of the firm's vision and strategy to ensure that they are stated in ways that lend themselves to alignment. For example, a useful vision statement describes the company as it wishes to become in the future and includes steps that allow progress toward the vision to be measured. A vision that says the company wants to be the "best" in its industry is not particularly useful. "Best" in what terms? Revenue? Profits? Market share? Customer satisfaction? How is this progress to be measured?

Strategy

Once a useful vision is formulated, a firm must examine its strategy for achieving the vision. Is it generally known within the firm what the strategy is? Does it make sense in the context of the vision? Do the vision and the strategy seem aligned, that is, are they consistent and complementary? Does the strategy explain how the company intends to realize the vision?

If either the vision or the strategy is not stated in useful terms, they must be reformulated in a way that allows the company to measure progress toward achieving them. Once the vision is defined and the strategy outlined, a firm can begin to think about how intellectual capital can contribute, either in the value to be created for the firm or in the kind of value to be extracted. For some companies the role of intellectual capital is to create the innovations that will become the products and services of the future. In other companies, whose strategy is to add value through assembly or integration of components, the intellectual capital focuses on integrating the innovations of others and adding value through low-cost manufacturing or distribution. In still other companies, the intellectual capital may be integral to creating a reputation or image that the company uses to differentiate itself in its marketplace. The set of roles any one company selects for its intellectual capital depends largely on the kind of firm it is, its vision for itself, and the strategy it has chosen. The flow of thought for aligning the vision, strategy, and intellectual capital is displayed in Exhibit 2.2.

For example, at Xerox, which calls itself the "document company," the vision and strategy call upon the firm to recreate the concept of what a document is, through new technology. This business strategy establishes a relatively clear role for intellectual capital. The human capital will develop the technology and the innovations that will be used by the company as the basis for its products and services in the future. The business strategy tells the company what kind of new knowledge it

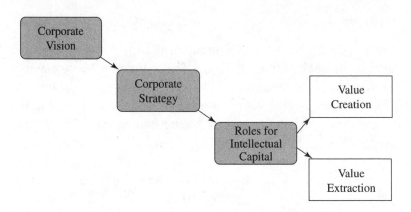

Exhibit 2.2   Determining the Roles for Intellectual Capital

must create (value creation). It also suggests that the company will be extracting value from its IC in two forms: revenue from future products and services, and in the reputation and image that result from its technological leadership. Both forms of value are the direct result of the efforts of the company's intellectual capital.

THE SECOND DIMENSION: NON-ACCOUNTING MODELS OF THE FIRM

The second dimension of the IC framework involves describing or modeling the firm in non-accounting terms. This portion of the framework uses graphic models to describe intellectual capital, IC companies, and some of the more important IC activities for knowledge firms. The second dimension provides us with the very essence of a knowledge company. Perhaps more importantly, it includes information that is key to understanding how knowledge companies convert innovations into value. The models contained in this dimension of the framework allow us to understand what the sources of value for knowledge companies are as well as the ways that value can be converted into cash.

Static Models of an IC Framework

The first two models describing the firm in non-accounting terms are static, that is, they don't have any moving parts. They are pictures that help us to visualize the answers to the following questions: What is intellectual capital? What are its major components or elements (see Exhibit 1.1)? What kind of company is concerned with intellectual capital? What are its major elements (see Exhibit 2.3)?

The definitions and graphic depictions of intellectual capital are useful for understanding what IC and knowledge firms are, but they do not help us understand how to manage a firm's intellectual capital. The dynamic portion of the framework is more helpful for this.

Dynamic Models of an IC Framework

The two dynamic models (meaning they contain movement or activity flow) help us to answer different questions: Is it possible to develop a set of activities that allow a firm to routinely extract value from its intellectual assets? If so, what are the elements of such a system (see Exhibit 2.5)? Is it possible to link activities associated with IC management with the firm's vision and strategy so that IC may contribute to the firm's success at achieving its vision through its chosen strategy (see Exhibit 2.2)?

Together the two static and two dynamic models of IC and IC management activities constitute the framework for viewing and evaluating how value is created and extracted. The models also offer insights into the firm's profitability that have not been available to knowledge company managers and executives before. The remainder of this chapter provides a more detailed discussion of each element of this framework.

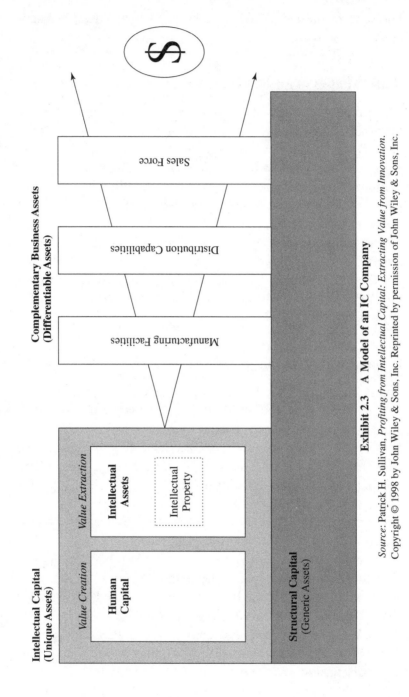

Exhibit 2.3   A Model of an IC Company

Source: Patrick H. Sullivan, *Profiting from Intellectual Capital: Extracting Value from Innovation.*
Copyright © 1998 by John Wiley & Sons, Inc. Reprinted by permission of John Wiley & Sons, Inc.

THE STRUCTURE OF KNOWLEDGE COMPANIES

Firms defined as knowledge companies are comprised of intellectual capital and structural capital, where the structural capital has two components: tangible assets and complementary business assets. In addition, each kind of capital or asset may be categorized as unique, differentiable, or generic.

Unique Assets

The intellectual capital of knowledge firms is a unique set of assets. No other firm has exactly the same set of skills, abilities, knowledge, innovations, codified knowledge, patents, trademarks, copyrights, and trade secrets. These assets are not only unique; they are also difficult to duplicate. If another firm wished to duplicate them it would take a considerable amount of time (and resources) to do so. As a practical matter, these assets are not duplicable in the short run.

Differentiable Assets

This class of assets is often not unique. It includes assets such as manufacturing and distribution, which while similar to those found in competing firms are different in some ways from those of competitors. For example, although all firms in the semiconductor industry have fabrication facilities, no two are alike. They differ in size, shape, complexity, production rate, and cost structure. The same is true for each firm's distribution capability as well as its sales capability. Although all firms in the semiconductor manufacturing business must have manufacturing, distribution, and sales capabilities, no two are alike. Together with a firm's unique assets, the differentiable assets make each firm different from its competitors. A special classification of differentiable assets is called the firm's complementary business assets. Complementary business assets (so named because they complement the firm's innovations) are important to knowledge firms for generating and maintaining profits. For a discussion of complementary business assets see the Appendix.

Generic Assets

This class of assets includes things that are generally not differentiable, such as cash, fixed capital, and tangible assets. Virtually all of the assets included in this category may be found on the firm's balance sheet.

A model of a knowledge firm is shown in Exhibit 2.3. As the exhibit shows, the complementary business assets act as a lens. They magnify the value of the firm's intellectual capital. We can think of the complementary business assets as a series of lenses, each of which magnifies the value that was produced by its predecessor. For example, an idea for a new product has value by itself. When embodied in the design of a product the idea becomes more valuable. Its value is increased once the product is manufactured, further increased when it is distributed and available for sale, and again when it is sold. At each step in this simple illustration, the complementary assets of the firm (manufacturing, distribution, sales) increase the value of the original innovative idea.

Looking at a knowledge company from this perspective allows a firm to ask itself: Where in the company is its value created? Does the company create its value through its intellectual capital, its differentiable tangible assets, or its generic tangible assets? What portion of the value created does each kind of asset produce? A company that knows the answer to that question can then examine how it allocates its resources. After all, a CEO should be concerned with allocating an appropriate level of resources to the portions of the firm that are the source of its value. If the firm is not doing so, the CEO needs to know why.

Many kinds of firms create a large portion of their value through their complementary business assets, so a major portion of their resources should be allocated to the activities associated with these value-producing assets (e.g., manufacturing, distribution, sales). Similarly, a firm that gets most of its value directly from its human capital should allocate a large portion of its assets to hiring, training, education, knowledge creation, and knowledge capture. Matching resources proportionally with the activities that produce the value is not a hard and fast rule. Nevertheless, firms should consider whether doing so will or will not produce greater benefits than other resource allocation mixes.

Dow Chemical, Eastman Chemical, and DuPont are examples of knowledge companies. With their acres of pipelines, towers, and distillation machinery, these companies have a major investment in fixed plant and equipment, but they use all of that hardware as the means to convert new ideas for molecules into products that are sold to customers. In that sense, they are classic knowledge companies.

Each of these companies can likely answer the following key questions:

- What percentage of my company's resources is allocated to unique assets? differentiated assets? generic assets?
- What percentage of my company's value is a result of its unique assets? differentiated assets? generic assets?
- How would I like my company to create value?
- Should my company reallocate the resources it devotes to unique assets? to differentiated assets? to generic assets?

ONE APPROACH TO EXTRACTING VALUE FROM A FIRM'S INTELLECTUAL CAPITAL

The economic literature is helpful in exploring the potential sources of value for knowledge companies. To date, economists have focused largely on value in the form of cash and have not dealt with the difficult-to-quantify value of strategic

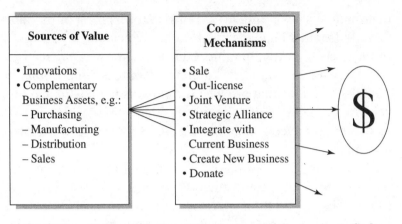

Exhibit 2.4   Sources of Value and Mechanisms for Conversion to Cash

Source: Patrick H. Sullivan, *Profiting from Intellectual Capital: Extracting Value from Innovation*. Copyright © 1998 by John Wiley & Sons, Inc. Reprinted by permission of John Wiley & Sons, Inc.

position. Exhibit 2.4 summarizes the current view of economists as to the sources of value for knowledge companies as well as the mechanisms available for converting that value into cash.

THE THIRD DIMENSION: IC ACTIVITIES

We have discussed the context that provides direction for the firm's intellectual capital (the first dimension) and the models describing the firm in a non-accounting manner (the second dimension). Now we can turn to the third dimension of the framework, the actions associated with extracting value from the firm's intellectual capital. This portion of the IC framework discussion focuses on how companies extract value from their IC in an operational sense. What activities, procedures, software tools, and policies are used to convert ideas into value for the corporation? The intellectual asset management system (IAMS) described below is nothing more than a set of activities (decisions, decision processes, information-gathering, and work processes), organized into a common-sense flow or process, that companies use to systematically evaluate and extract value from their intellectual assets. Because it reflects the collective learning of some two dozen companies, there is no one company that uses the system exactly as it is defined here. Yet if they were able to begin all over again, each would likely choose a system with the following components (see Exhibit 2.5).

The Innovation Process

All firms have their own approach and method for developing new or innovative ideas that create value. For many technology companies the innovation process is an R&D (research and development) activity; service companies, on the other hand, often have a creativity department; still others rely on their employees in the field to produce innovative ideas. Whatever the firm's source of new innovations, the generic system calls this the innovation process.

Portfolio Inclusion: The Go/No-Go Decision

Most firms have a method for evaluating the new ideas that emerge from the innovation process. Innovations that pass the screening—those that are deemed likely to be useful to the company in pursuit of its strategy—are selected for inclusion in the company's portfolio of intellectual assets. Some companies use the screening process to determine which innovations will be patented (the decision to patent requires an investment of up to $200,000 to obtain and maintain legal protection for an innovation for its twenty-year life). This decision is important for all companies because it separates ideas that are of particular interest to the firm from ideas that, though they may be good and interesting, are not aligned with the firm's strategy. (When a firm decides *not* to patent, it often maintains an innovation in

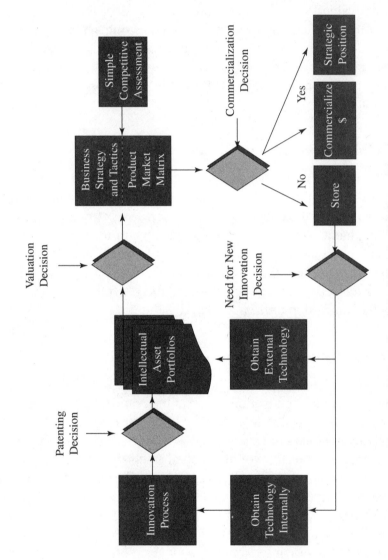

Exhibit 2.5   A System for Managing Intellectual Assets

the know-how of its employees; sometimes formally protecting this knowledge as a trade secret.)

The Intellectual Asset Portfolio

The portfolio is in fact a series of portfolios containing the firm's different kinds of intellectual assets. Some of the portfolios may contain intellectual properties; others may contain documents of potential business interest (e.g.: customer lists, price lists, business practices, and internal processes); and still others may contain ideas or innovations that are in the portfolio because of their potential to create profits.

Coarse Valuation of Opportunity

Each innovation of potential interest should be valued before it is reviewed for use. Valuation in this sense is a bifurcated process. The first part of the valuation process is to narratively describe how the intellectual asset is expected to bring value to the firm. Following this qualitative valuation, the firm should attempt to quantify, where possible, the amount of value it expects the innovation to provide.

A Simple Competitive Assessment

While competitive assessments in business are commonplace, the competitive assessment contemplated here is focused on the intellectual assets of the competition. In the case of technology companies, that focus might be on a competitor's technology as well as on its portfolio of patents.

Business Strategy / Tactics / Product-Market Mix

This portion of the intellectual asset management system involves a review of intellectual assets of interest matched with the firm's business strategy, tactics, and product-market mix.

The outcome of this review is an assessment of the fit between this asset and the organization's strategy, and a decision about how to use or dispose of the intellectual asset under review.

The Disposition Decision Process

The decision concerning the disposition of reviewed intellectual assets may have several possible outcomes. The intellectual asset may be commercialized or stored until another innovation is developed that makes the first one more marketable.

The Commercialization Decision Process

This process results in a decision about which of the conversion-to-cash mechanism(s) (shown in Exhibit 2.4) will be used to convert the innovation to cash.

Deciding Where to Seek Innovation

This decision process is invoked where it has been decided that a new innovation should be sought to add to an existing innovation to make the first more marketable. In this case, the question is whether to seek the new innovation from inside or outside the company (through in-licensing, acquisition of a company, etc.).

HOW TO USE THE IC FRAMEWORK

This framework is particularly useful for firms interested in creating or significantly improving their firm's capability for extracting value. Whereas Chapter 12 contains a complete discussion of how companies can fully implement systems and methods for extracting the optimum amount of value from their intellectual capital, the following outlines a few highlights to illustrate how to utilize the framework described in this chapter.

BEGIN WITH VISION AND STRATEGY

The company's view of itself in the future is a powerful symbol that can guide decision makers in the day-to-day detail of their jobs. Few companies have a well-articulated or well-written statement of vision, although for most companies there is an implicit understanding of what the firm sees as its future. In a similar fashion, most companies do not codify and widely distribute their business strategy. (Some companies believe that to do so would be to give away important strategic or tactical intelligence information to competitors. The truth is usually that competitors already know this information while the firm's own employees do not!)

Making the vision and strategy explicit, writing them down, and widely distributing them within the firm is a required early step in using the IC framework.

Manage the IP Portfolio

Intellectual property is one of the best-known of all of a firm's intangible assets (IP is comprised of patents, copyrights, trademarks, and trade secrets). For companies with one or more portfolios of these intellectual properties, the place to begin is with the best-defined portfolio, typically the patent portfolio.

Define the Portfolio

What does it contain? Are the patents known? Surprisingly, many companies cannot even create a list of the patents they own.

Design the Intellectual Property Management System (IPMS)

Describe the IPMS the firm ultimately wishes to create. Include the basic functional elements as well as the decision processes and their supporting work processes and databases. The system design at this stage should be at the overview level. (Detailed design plans at this early stage are not necessary and could even be a nonproductive diversion.) The overview IPMS design developed here becomes the template for a more detailed system to be developed at a later date.

Design the Portfolio Database

Effective patent management demands that there be both a hard copy of each patent and a computer file containing useful information on each patent which is needed for decisions at several levels: management of patents as legal documents, management of patents as business assets, tactical business decisions, and strategic business decisions.

Establish the Competitive Assessment Activity

An understanding of the competition is vital to managing the firm's intellectual property. Each firm needs to know what both its business and its technology competitors have produced, what their current positions and capabilities are, and what actions can be expected from them in the future. Competitive assessment should be performed by people with business as well as technical backgrounds. Many technology firms try to use technologists as business analysts on the mistaken assumption that business analysis is relatively easy for those with a scientific or analytical background. But competent and effective business analysis requires the kind of special training found in business or economics programs at universities. Anything less than this level of training is not recommended.

Create a Patent Policy for the Firm

In an ideal world, businesses would only develop innovations that are in line with their strategy or that would enable their vision. In our less-than-ideal real world, innovators produce what they produce, and these innovations are not all necessarily on target for the vision or the strategy. To make decision-making easier, a policy that establishes guidelines for what the firm wishes to patent is desirable. Patent policies span the range of possibilities:

- Patent in order to have a portfolio with which to negotiate business agreements (licenses, joint ventures, alliances, and so forth) with other companies.
- After a brief examination, patent most things that have a chance of technical success.
- After careful scrutiny, patent only those discoveries that have a strong chance of technical success regardless of potential business application or use.
- Patent only those discoveries that have a clear application to your own company's products or processes.
- Patent discoveries that might block or delay similar discoveries by competitors.
- Patent most things that are patentable.
- Patent only the occasional discovery of quite exceptional importance.
- Do not patent anything.

Regularize the Patent Generation Process

All technology firms have a process of some kind that produces innovations targeted for patenting. Not all of the innovations produced are of patentable quality; and even if they were, the firm might not wish to invest in patenting them. While the patenting policy provides one level of decision-making guidance, many more innovations clear the policy guideline hurdle than the firm may wish to patent. The decision to patent is best made after considering the firm's business strategy, the dollar amount of budget it has reserved to cover the costs of patenting, and the set of patentable innovations available for consideration.

Firms that wish to ensure an adequate flow of innovations create internal systems for communicating information about innovations being developed. These allow firms to know whether sufficient numbers of innovations are in progress to meet their strategic needs, whether too many are in progress in one technology area and not enough in another, or whether too few innovations are in progress overall. The firm's existing processes for knowing what is in the pipeline and for making the patent decision should be regularized and perhaps made more efficient. Such a regularization will allow the firm to know that it has a sufficient number and quality of innovations to meet its needs.

Develop a Valuation Process

Before investing in the extraction of value from an intangible asset it is a good idea to determine its relative value to the firm. If it is capable of producing only a small amount of value, it may not be worth the firm's energies or investment. If, on the other hand, it represents a large amount of potential value, the firm will be eager to invest in extracting its value. To make this determination, firms should create the capability for people within the organization to evaluate both the quality and the monetary value of the firm's intellectual assets. The capability should include a range of valuation methods providing dollar values ranging from coarse valuation to fine.

Develop a Value-Extraction Analysis Capability

For each technology with the potential for commercialization, several questions must be asked and answered before the company can decide to invest in commercialization. For example, which combination of conversion mechanisms should the firm use to extract the most value from the innovation? Each technology requires an analysis to determine how many of the conversion mechanisms the firm can use to obtain the best profit results from the innovation.

Create a Licensing/Joint Venture/Strategic Alliance Capability

Once the firm has decided to commercialize an innovation, it needs the capability to make the commercialization happen. In many cases this means commercializing the innovation through licensing, joint venturing, or entering into a strategic alliance. Firms must develop an office or a capability that will be able to expeditiously develop a license, joint venture, or strategic alliance agreement and execute it for the firm.

Move Up to Managing Intellectual Assets

At this point, a firm that has created the foregoing capabilities has largely developed a systematic approach to managing its intellectual property. Firms that want to expand their system to include intellectual assets (the non-legally-protected, codified, profit-producing knowledge of the firm) may do so relatively easily by expanding the capability of the IPMS.

Develop Portfolios of Non-Protected Assets

Create defined portfolios (and databases) for intellectual assets with commercial possibilities. The list of portfolios of nonprotected assets might include licenses (both in- and out-licenses), nondisclosure agreements, joint venture agreements, outsourcing contracts and service agreements, IA aspects of mergers and acquisitions, customer lists, price lists, business practices, and internal processes.

Develop IP Linkages Between Portfolios

Identify linkages between the IA portfolio databases. These might include company names, individuals' names, technologies, and products or services.

Expand the Competitive Assessment Capability

Although a competitive assessment capability focused on intellectual property has already been developed as part of the IPMS, moving to the IA level usually requires a firm to increase the capability level of its competitive assessment activities. This increased capability may include expanding the information-gathering activity to obtain information about the marketplace positions and long-term strategies of competitors; learning more about competitors' activities, such as strategic arrangements with other firms and outsourcing arrangements; and upgrading the ability to determine the specific value of the firm's own current and potential portfolio based on its effect on competitors (e.g., infringements and design-arounds, as well as predicted competitor response to potential strategic thrusts).

Create a Litigation-Avoidance Capability

Companies need to know how to determine whether they are infringing on another's intellectual property rights and, equally, whether another company might be infringing on theirs. Information about written agreements of all kinds, including nondisclosure agreements, contracts, and agreements with suppliers, when correlated, contributes to viable litigation avoidance capability.

Managing the Firm's Intellectual Capital

Firms that manage their intellectual capital effectively are strategically focused on managing all three forms of IC: human capital, intellectual assets, and intellectual property. For technology companies, the creation of an IP/IA management system means that the building blocks are in place, but non-technology companies need to ensure that a competitive assessment of human capital is in existence as well.

Whereas the technology company's competitive assessment focuses on the business and technology competitors, the non-technology company must focus on its competitors' human capital.

In addition to the capabilities discussed heretofore for IP and IA management systems, non-technology firms need to develop the following new capabilities:

A Human Capital Management Strategy

In the management of the firm's human capital, it is important to know the current and ideal use of the human resource. What is the ideal allocation or alignment of the firm's human capital for achieving the near-term goals? Long-term goals? What is the actual current alignment? What is the value-creation focus of the human capital? What is the know-how the human capital has created? How is this know-how defined? How may it be described? What is the firm's ability to access it? What is the firm's ability to commercialize it? What systems are in place or can be developed to manage the firm's human capital?

A Human Capital Measurement Capability

How does the firm define, describe, and measure its intellectual capital? What kinds of knowledge does the firm's human capital (HC) generate? What is the breadth and depth of knowledge created?

A Reporting System

What kinds of reports does the firm have or wish to have about its intellectual capital? Internal reports? Actual or potential external reports? Do these include measures of key IC activities? Do they include valuations of the firm's human capital?

SUMMARY

This chapter has described a three-dimensional IC framework that reveals the IC aspects of the firm. It allows us to determine what is important to the firm and, thereby, to differentiate foreground from background. A firm that uses this framework may more easily identify the portions of the firm that produce the major elements of its value and discover how to extract that value for the benefit of the firm. By providing a set of common-sense steps to follow in creating or improving the firm's ability to extract value from intellectual properties, intellectual assets, and human capital, the framework should also be useful for firms wanting to improve their ability to manage and extract value from their IC.

3

Linking Intellectual
Capital with Value

With the framework for understanding intellectual capital and knowledge companies now in place we can turn to the next question: What is the link between an innovation (knowledge that can be converted into profit) and value for the corporation? This question has bedeviled anyone who believes in the value of intellectual capital. For such believers this linkage has been an article of faith, but believers often lament the difficulty of convincing the skeptics. Skeptics frequently demand some sort of proof of the value of intangibles, such as the dollar amount of sales attributable to intellectual capital or profit figures, but because most of the value IC brings to a firm is indirect, through its effect on one or more company activities, IC usually cannot be directly linked to the realization of corporate value. The link is therefore often difficult to identify, much less to quantify.

Suppose a company had a menu from which it could order certain kinds of value. What would be included on such a menu? Would the items be categorized in IC-related groups, like appetizers, entrees, and desserts? What would the categories be? What would be listed in each one? To explore this idea I asked the member companies in the ICM Gathering for assistance.

THE VALUE BROUGHT BY IC

At a 1999 meeting of the ICM Gathering, the member companies listed the following values of intellectual capital to their companies:

- Product and services revenue
- Reputation and image
- Access to the technology of others
- Litigation avoidance
- Design freedom
- Reduced costs
- Blocked competition
- Barriers to entry by potential competitors
- Customer loyalty
- Protection for innovations

Direct vs. Indirect Value

It should be obvious that intellectual capital provides firms with two kinds of value. The most direct is cash flow. As the fundamental driver of a firm's cash flow, the intellectual capital of the firm creates the innovations that are subsequently converted into revenue (and other kinds of value). In addition, the firm's intellectual capital determines how the firm will conduct its business in a cost-effective manner. Because the firm's intellectual capital creates its income and manages its cost streams, IC is a primary generator of the firm's profits.

The second kind of value is less direct. Some firms use their intellectual capital to position themselves strategically. Their IC is evidence of their intellectual leadership and can be a basis for their customer loyalty. Other firms use the size and power of their patent portfolios to intimidate competing or copycat firms that might otherwise file lawsuits claiming rights to an innovation. Still other firms use their portfolio of intellectual capital assets as a bargaining chip in business negotiations.

Direct-value activities are those that provide an unambiguous link between intellectual capital and value, either revenue or profit. Any intellectual capital activity that results in revenue or cost reduction is considered a direct-value activity. Thus, a direct-value activity (1) can be explicitly linked to the vision or strategy; (2) deals with revenue or cost; and (3) is easily measured.

Indirect-value activities, in contrast, cannot be directly linked to vision, strategy, revenue, or cost, and they are not easily measured. The links between the activities and the value they produce, while often intuitively obvious and sometimes compelling, are not associated with a transaction (such as a sale). A transaction is an event that signifies a transition from one state to another; it typically includes the payment of a market price. Indirect-value activities are not associated with transactions and are therefore less clearly linked and measured.

Offensive and Defensive Value

Some kinds of IC-related value have defensive dimensions; others have offensive dimensions.

Defensive activity prepares the firm for invasive action by individuals or groups outside of the firm. Its purpose is preparation and its focus is on developing assets or resources that will help repel or neutralize intrusive activities that threaten some aspects of the firm's vision or strategy. Defensive activity is generally viewed as passive in nature.

Offensive activity targets individuals or groups outside the firm. Its purpose is to advance the organization's ability to achieve its strategic vision or to implement its strategy. The activity frequently concerns revenue and profit generation.

49

Type of Activity	Direct Value	Indirect Value
Offensive	Revenue or sales Access to the technology of others	Enforcement of legal rights
Defensive		Obtaining legal protection Litigation avoidance Design freedom
Offensive & Defensive	Cost reduction activities (manufacturing, distribution, sales, marketing)	Reputation/image Blocking competition Barriers to entry Customer loyalty Being a player

Exhibit 3.1   The Value of IC to Corporations

Let's return to the list provided in the first section of this chapter. As you can see, some intellectual capital management activities are neither entirely defensive nor entirely offensive but a mixture of both (see Exhibit 3.1).

A MENU FOR VALUE

Different kinds of IC produce different kinds of value (see Exhibit 3.2). Not surprisingly, the value associated with the more concrete of the intangibles (intellectual properties and intellectual assets) is the easiest to define and measure, whereas the value associated with the softer kinds of intellectual capital (know-how and relationships) is less easy to define, describe, and measure.

Let us review each kind of IC highlighted in Exhibit 3.2 and the kinds of value it is capable of bringing to the corporation. The data in this exhibit is drawn from the IC Gathering companies, who stated that four kinds of IC brought the most

Defensive	Patents	Trademarks	Know-how	Relationships
	• Protection (exclude others) • Design Freedom	• Protection (exclude others)	• Protection (trade secret)	

Offensive	Patents	Trademarks	Know-how	Relationships
Revenue	• Products and Services (P&S), Sale, License, Joint Venture (JV), Strategic Alliance (SA), Integrate, Donate • Patents: Sale, License, Donate	• P&S: Sales • TM: Sale, License	• Sell, License, JV, SA, Integrate	• P&S: Sales
Cost	• Litigation Avoidance • Access the Technology of Others	• Litigation Avoidance • Access the Technology of Others	• Litigation Avoidance	• Reduced Marketing Costs
Position	• Reputation/Image • Competitive Blocking • Barrier to Competition	• Name Recognition • Customer Loyalty • Barrier to Competition	• Reputation/Image • Barrier to Entry	• Reputation/Image • Customer Loyalty • Barrier to Entry

P&S = Products and Services; SA = Strategic Alliance; JV = Joint Venture; TM = Trademark

Exhibit 3.2 IC Value Matrix

value to their companies: patents, trademarks, know-how, and relationships.

Value Associated with Patents

Patents bring both defensive and offensive value to their owners.

Defensive Value

Mere ownership of patents implies defensive activity. Patent protection conveys the right to exclude others from unauthorized use of the intellectual asset that is protected. Such rights are defensive (and indirect) in nature.

Offensive Value

Patents provide their owners with a range of potential offensive uses. In providing an owner with rights to an exclusive use of a technology, a patent may be used to generate revenue in the following ways: from the direct sale of the products and services protected by the patent, from licensing rights to the products and services, from joint ventures associated with producing products and services, or from strategic alliances formed to reach new markets for the products or services. A company may also donate a patent in order to receive tax benefits as demonstrated by the following examples. IBM has generated over $1 billion per year in licensing revenue. Dow Chemical proudly claims that it has surpassed its goal of $125 million in annual licensing revenue, with this form of income still growing. Some companies are bringing together all of their patents under one organization, sometimes a separately formed company, to optimize their commercialization (Bell South and Sonoco are two current examples). When patents are used to generate revenue, their value is offensive and direct.

Patents may also be used to lower company costs. For example, a patent that is well-written and valid may dramatically reduce the possibility that its owner will be sued for patent infringement. High-quality patents can be a key factor in minimizing a company's litigation costs. Where cost reduction is the value to be extracted from patents, this value is considered to be direct. Patents may also be used as bargaining chips to obtain access to the technology of others. Patents are often more valuable than cash when a competitor needs access to a technology owned by another firm. Technology competitors may be able to establish licensing agreements when other forms of negotiation fail.

Some companies use patented technologies as measures of a reputation or image in the marketplace. For example, IBM, 3M, Texas Instruments, Hewlett-Packard, and Xerox are all companies whose reputations rest on their ability to provide customers with products based upon the latest and best technology. These companies all have substantial portfolios of high-quality patents. Their portfolios bolster their image of technology leadership, which helps them compete in their respective marketplaces. A company that cannot achieve technology leadership may seek instead to be a "standard setter" or simply a "player." In some industries, in order to be considered a "player" a company needs bargaining chips to bring to the table—in other words, evidence that it is able to play in the game. A portfolio of high-quality patents is such evidence.

Patents may also be used to block competitors from certain kinds of technology initiatives that would intrude on a patent owner's business or market. Competitive blocking is one often-used value of patents.

Value Associated with Trademarks

Trademarks, the marks or brands that companies use to identify themselves or their products in the marketplace, are another form of legal protection. Trademarking, or legally protecting a brand, means preventing others from using it.

Defensive Value

The defensive value of a trademark is that others may not use it without the express permission of the holder of the rights to the mark. A company may use its trademark to differentiate itself and its products in the marketplace.

Offensive Value

Products and services sold under a trademark often command premium prices, particularly when the trademark is viewed by the purchaser as a guarantee of quality. When a trademark becomes widely known and the products associated with it are highly regarded, competitors without trademark recognition may suffer in the marketplace. Name recognition may lead to repeat sales as well as convoyed sales, thereby reducing a firm's marketing cost per sale. (Convoyed sales are sales of other company products or services after a "first" purchase of a company product. For example, the purchaser of a particular brand of television may decide to purchase a VCR made by the same manufacturer. In this case the VCR would be considered a convoyed sale.)

At least one company has tried to use its trademark to extend the franchise it received through its patent. Nutrasweet is reported to have made significant efforts to ensure that its swirl trademark would appear on all products containing Nutrasweet, realizing that the patent protection for Aspertame (the chemical sweetener itself) would expire at the end of its patent period. The Nutrasweet people have tried to ensure that there is now enough value, or customer loyalty, to the trademark that the mark itself will continue to guarantee a high rate of sales for products on which it appears.

Cost-Reduction Value

Like patents, trademarks that are well protected reduce the probability of costly litigation or legal disputes about owner-ship rights or rights to use the mark.

Positioning Value

In providing name recognition for a company and its products, a trademark may be sufficient incentive for a consumer to buy a new product from a company whose trademark it trusts. Related to name recognition is customer loyalty. Consumers who proudly proclaim that they would never buy any brand of car other than, say, a Ford, are important customers; and companies spend significant amounts of money to foster such loyalty to a brand name. Other companies use their advertise-ments to encourage loyalty: "Have It Your Way" is the slogan of one fast-food chain that wants its customers to know that they can buy a "customized" product. "I Want My MTV" is another slogan designed to create customer loyalty.

Barriers to Competition

Companies with well-branded or trademarked products may often "own" a market. Consider the market for aspirin. While it is common knowledge that aspirin is the same, no matter who makes it, the relatively small number of companies that manu-facture and sell aspirin go out of their way to differentiate their aspirin through their brands. A new entrant into the aspirin market would face the formidable barrier of having to compete with several worldwide trademarks.

Value Associated with Human Capital

Human capital, the source and repository of all tacit knowl-edge, is generally considered to include three different kinds of intellectual capital: knowledge and know-how, relationships, and organizational capital. The following paragraphs highlight several ways in which knowledge or know-how and relationships provide value to their organizations. The state of the art for determining the value associated with organizational capital is the least advanced of the three forms of tacit knowledge and is not dealt with in detail here.

Knowledge/Know-How

Know-how, generally considered to be tacit, may be explicit—that is, it may be definable and describable but still reside in a tacit form. Some service companies, such as law firms and consulting firms, sell access to their employees' knowledge or know-how. Some manufacturing firms also obtain value from the know-how of their employees in ways other than through its direct commercialization. Employees with very specific skills—how to operate complicated machinery or install and set up a factory, for example—possess knowledge or know-how that can be converted into value.

Explicit Know-How.   This is knowledge that a firm knows its employees have. As a defensive tactic, a firm may legally register its employees' knowledge as a trade secret. This means that a company has exclusive rights to the use of this knowledge as long as the company follows certain procedures to protect it and to restrict access to it. Other individuals and organizations may not use knowledge that is a trade secret.

A firm's know-how may provide offensive value by reducing costs or creating a positive image for the firm. For example, companies whose know-how is well documented in the form of trade secrets or where the know-how is unique to the corporation or widely known to be held by the corporation, find themselves less likely to be the target of litigation. Know-how may also help a firm position its image or reputation. Perhaps one of the most famous bits of know-how is the formula

56

for Coca-Cola. Know-how is also often used as a credential for companies that want to become "players" in an industry. Know-how can sometimes be as important as patents or explicit knowledge.

Tacit Know-How. This is know-how that is not explicitly known. It has virtually no defensive value. The fact that it is not explicitly known means that it has no potential for legal protection as a trade secret. Also, in cases where it is not explicit what the know-how may be, it has little value in litigation avoidance. The major value that firms with tacit know-how may enjoy is often in the field of reputation or image. When a firm is known to have a large amount of know-how, even though it may not be explicitly known in detail what it is, the existence of the know-how as a capability is often sufficient to provide the firm with a desirable reputation.

Value Associated with Relationships

The value residing within relationships has only recently been formally recognized and is not yet fully understood. Hubert St. Onge (see Appendix, "A Brief History of the ICM Movement") was among the first to popularize the notion and the importance of customer capital. The new idea that customers are a form of capital was attractive and almost electrifying in its simplicity and implications for the firm. People could immediately grasp the concept of customer capital and think through how they and their firm might benefit from it. Some call this "relationship capital."

The course of doing business involves maintaining a large number of relationships both inside and outside the firm. Internal relationships are those between and among individuals and groups. From the value perspective, important internal relationships are those that enhance the firm's ability to create the value that it subsequently wishes to extract.

Whereas internal relationships tend to focus on the creation of value, external relationships are more concerned with the extraction of that value. Examples of external relationships are those with customers, suppliers, and investors. Customer relationships, or customer capital, are defined by St. Onge as having four dimensions: the depth (penetration), the width (coverage), the attachment (loyalty), and the profitability of the company's franchise. The ICM Gathering companies report that customer relationships are valuable when they either reduce the cost of marketing or increase the number of repeat sales, convoyed sales, or long-term sales. In any event, the relationship that a firm has with its customers can and does bring value to the firm as measured by sales and costs.

Good relationships between a firm and its suppliers are mutually supportive and beneficial and have distinct advantages for both. In many cases these relationships lead to reduced costs and increased assurance of supply for the company. They also mean reduced marketing costs and assurance of revenue for the supplier. The degree to which a firm can work with its suppliers to create more mutual value is the degree to which it can create more and closer attachments and mutual loyalties. These kinds of relationships, properly considered, become relationships that enhance the firm's profits and performance.

Asset Allocation and Value

A case can be made for the leverage that is obtainable through unique combinations of tangible and intangible assets. Proponents of this position argue that by putting together the "right" combination of assets, companies can create and sustain strategic position. This asset allocation view of a company maintains that one can determine a "best" proportion of a company's physical assets (raw materials, buildings, and equipment), intellectual capital (ideas, systems, processes, and culture), internal relationships (employees and suppliers) and external relationships (customers and investors). Further, this view holds that how a company builds and manages its portfolio of such assets determines its success.

Arthur Andersen has invested significant resources in developing a set of approaches for companies interested in asset allocation strategies. Their approach is that companies are comprised of assets—tangible and intangible—and that these assets drive value creation. The Arthur Andersen approach to the creation of corporate value, called "Value Dynamics," holds that companies create value by assembling unique combinations of assets and that the company's business model is the portfolio of such assets in which it has invested.[1]

SUMMARY

This chapter has discussed the kinds of value that intellectual capital provides to the firm, including direct and indirect, offensive and defensive, and internal and external value. Although these different kinds of value have now been made explicit, the link between the basic innovation that is the source of the value and the realization of that value has not yet been defined. Two further questions remain: How does a firm identify the activities within the firm that make the IC value appear? How does a firm manage and measure progress toward achieving the anticipated value?

NOTE

1. Boulton, R., E. Ginault, B. Libert, *Value Dynamics*, New York: HarperCollins, January 2000.

4

IC Value Chains

In the previous chapter we learned that there are a number of ways in which intellectual capital may bring value to the corporation. But just knowing about the kind of value to extract from intellectual capital isn't enough to make it happen. In addition, we need to know what *activities* must be managed to make it happen. IC activities, the third dimension of the IC framework, and knowing how to manage them is at the core of extracting the desired value.

To briefly recap, we know how to determine where the company is headed (its vision and strategy), how to view the company from an IC perspective, and how to extract value from its intellectual assets (sources of value and conversion mechanisms). In Chapter 3 we learned about the kinds of value that firms are able to extract from their intellectual capital. We also learned that this value should be well defined so that it can be accurately measured. Producing the desired value from the firm's intellectual assets is the focus of this chapter.

Given the day-to-day detail of managing resources and processes, how does the IA manager know which ones are more important than others? How does he or she decide where to focus the firm's resources in order to realize the most IC value? In addition, firms expect to realize more than one kind of IC value, each requiring a different set of activities, the chapter also discusses how managers can prioritize their resource allocation decisions.

THE IC VALUE CHAIN

In the context of intellectual capital, an IC value chain is a set of required activities that span the space between the moment of innovation and the realization of value.

In the past, when a manufacturing firm's IC devised a new innovation for a product, the innovation was first codified (committed to paper or some form of media). The codified innovation was then reviewed and patented (to protect it and to prevent other companies from using it). Once protected, the product was manufactured, distributed, and finally sold. The value chain for moving the innovation from conception to incorporation in something of value is shown in Exhibit 4.1.

The Importance of IC Value Chains

CEOs of knowledge companies must be able to answer questions peculiar to these kinds of companies, a large portion of whose value is related to the firm's *intellectual* capital rather than to its tangible capital. For example:

- What value can and should the firm be realizing from its intellectual capital?
- How can the firm measure its progress toward realizing that value?

Exhibit 4.1   The "Old" IC Value Chain

- What can the firm do to extract that value? What are the activities involved?
- Which of these activities, if any, are more important to the firm than the others?
- What bottlenecks or operational difficulties does the firm need to resolve to improve its value extraction processes?
- Are resources optimally allocated to ensure that the firm is getting the best possible results from its intellectual capital?

The answers to these questions have eluded most knowledge companies, yet they are crucial to a knowledge firm's ability to maximize the value of its intellectual capital.

Answering the Significant Questions

We already know, for example, that it is possible for a firm to determine the kinds of value it wishes to extract from its intellectual capital. Chapter 3 described and discussed the many kinds of value possible to realize from IC, as well as the importance of developing measures that define success and progress toward success. What remains to be identified are the management requirements and the activities associated with creating value. The following steps will help to identify both:

1. For each kind of IC value desired, determine the value chain activities, that is, the activities that are associated with value extraction:
   - IC management activities
   - Other activities
2. Focusing on IC management activities, determine the relative importance of the ICM activities.
   - Frequency of activity
   - Relative importance of the activity to value extraction

3. Describe and analyze the implications of the value chain.
  • Bottlenecks to be opened
  • Capabilities needed
  • Inefficiencies to be overcome
  • Resource reallocations called for
4. Set up an action plan.

Value Chain Activities

The activities shown in Exhibit 4.1 are so broad in scope that they are not useful when we want to understand the relationship between innovation and corporate value. A more detailed set of company activities (and one that is focused on the firm's IC management activities) would be more helpful to explain this linkage.

The advent of the intellectual capital management perspective has allowed us to better understand all of the activities associated with extracting value from one or more innovations. For example, there is now a widely agreed-upon generic system for managing intellectual assets. This decision system, discussed in Chapter 2, is reviewed here as Exhibit 4.2. This system makes it clear that there are distinct activities associated with transforming an innovation into something that brings value to the corporation.

The generic system for managing intellectual assets may also be viewed as a flow of the activities necessary for extracting value and as a basis for defining the activities in an IC value chain. A manufacturing firm, for example, may convert a new idea for a product into cash revenue as shown in Exhibit 4.3 (the shaded activities are those included in the IA management system shown in Exhibit 4.2).

The value chain in Exhibit 4.3 has "sell" as its desired end-value. Sell is a value measured in dollars of revenue from the products that incorporate the innovations created by the firm's

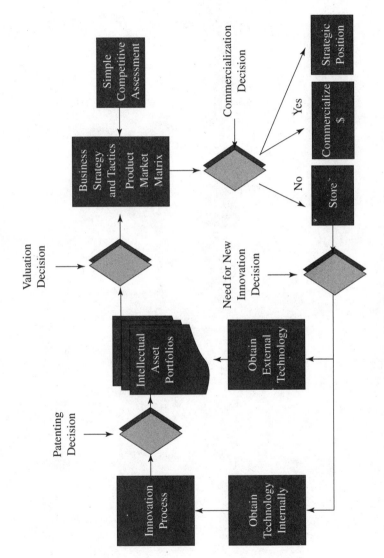

Exhibit 4.2   A Generic System for Managing Intellectual Assets

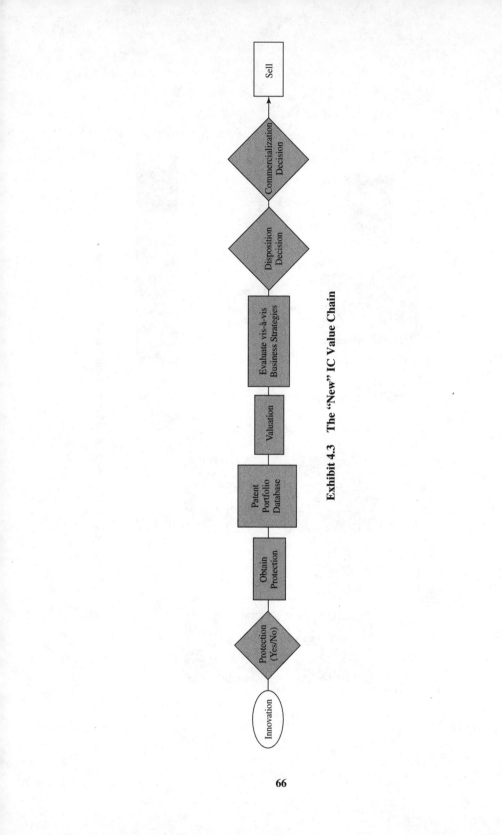

Exhibit 4.3 The "New" IC Value Chain

intellectual capital. (A more complicated analysis could determine how much revenue is associated with the innovation and how much can be attributed to the contributions from manufacturing, distribution, etc.)

EXAMPLES OF IC VALUE CHAINS

Suppose a manufacturing firm believes that the major value of its IC is in its *trademark*. How does the company measure the value it expects to obtain from its trademark? What kind of value does it want to obtain? What are the units of measurement? What are the standards? Also, how does the company create a value chain of the activities associated with realizing this value?

Firms may derive value from a trademark in several ways. For purposes of illustration, let us say that a manufacturing firm differentiates itself from its competitors by producing higher-quality products. By associating its products with a trademark, the firm may charge a premium price for all the products it sells.

Once the value desired by the firm has been identified and measures of success have been defined, the firm may turn its attention to the intellectual capital activities involved with producing the value and the portion of the IC value chain associated with obtaining premium prices for the company's products. Using the intellectual asset management system as our basis, the value chain for charging premium prices through the use of the company's trademark probably looks like Exhibit 4.4.

Another example of the value a firm may extract from its trademarks is *name recognition*. Name recognition (one form of what is sometimes called relationship capital) value comes from two different sets of activities: those associated with creating and maintaining the trademark and those associated with reaching a targeted population of consumers. Before we can know what activities will produce the desired result, we must determine how to measure name recognition. If name recogni-

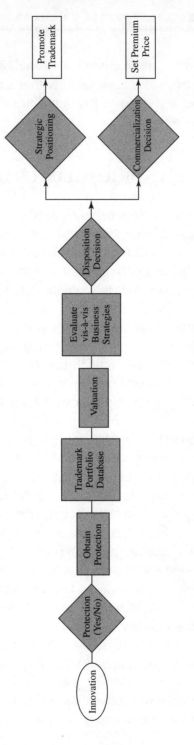

Exhibit 4.4   A Value Chain for Extracting Trademark Value

tion could be measured by a telephone survey of preselected target customers, the firm could develop a set of activities associated with producing that result. The activities associated with extracting name recognition value from the trademark set of intellectual properties are shown in Exhibit 4.5.

To further illustrate the point, assume that the manufacturing company also believed that maintaining good relationships with customers would reduce its marketing costs. Such a company would want to know which activities on the value chain would be associated with maintaining good relationships and also with reducing marketing costs. Such a value chain might look like Exhibit 4.6.

There are a number of similarities between the value chain in Exhibit 4.6 and the three preceding ones. There are also some notable differences. First, in the case of relationship capital, there is no innovation to launch the value chain; it is initiated by the relationships that the firms' employees and the firm itself has with customers. Second, there is no legal protection available for the firms' relationships. Relationships are not legally protectable; they are "protected" by their strength and by their ability to produce value for both the customer and the manufacturing firm. Third, the evaluation step involves creating a marketing plan specifying how the relationships with customers will be used to reduce marketing costs. Next, rather than a commercialization activity, this value chain calls for implementing, measuring, and monitoring the results of the marketing activity. Finally, the value realized by this activity is captured by the reduction of the firm's marketing costs.

Suppose that a manufacturing firm wants to minimize the costs of protecting its intellectual properties, particularly the costs associated with litigation, which typically includes the costs of litigation itself and any costs the firm might be required to pay in damages as an outcome of litigation. A value chain of activities to reduce litigation costs must first describe what value is sought and how that value is to be measured. In this case the value sought is cost savings or money-not-spent on litigation.

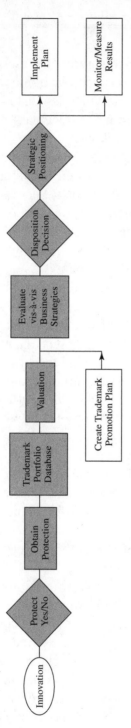

Exhibit 4.5 A Value Chain for Extracting Name Recognition Value

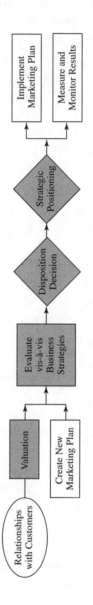

Exhibit 4.6 Value Chain for Extracting Relationship Value

At the beginning of a budget year the IP department of a firm might be required to estimate its litigation costs (including potential damages in lawsuits that could be decided against the company), as well as an estimate of cost savings goals, which could be achieved by more closely monitoring litigation activities, settling some lawsuits, or winning others.

Once the measure of results is determined, it is possible to create a value chain of activities that will produce the desired result and to describe the measures that can be used to assess the results of these activities. In this case, the litigation avoidance activity has several time dimensions: immediate, near term, and longer term.

1. For the *immediate* time frame the firm must be concerned with the management of immediate expenditures as well as monitoring the net profit value (NPV) of the potential outcomes of litigation.

2. Managing litigation costs for the *near term* involves creating a strong IP portfolio that will scare off potential litigants. The tasks associated with managing the input to the portfolio usually center on generating inventions that are focused on areas of business or legal interest, selecting those that will lead to the strongest patents, and preparing and submitting patent applications.

3. Managing litigation costs for the *long term* requires the firm to evaluate its portfolio strategically, looking ahead several years at the kinds of products or services it wants to offer in order to determine the evolution of its patent position.

A value chain that reflects the three time dimensions and focuses on extracting value in the form of reduced litigation costs would look like Exhibit 4.7.

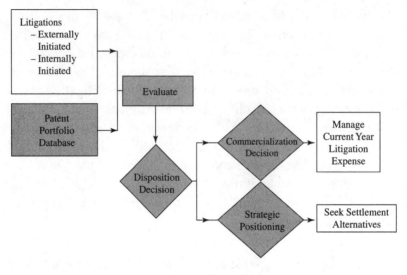

Exhibit 4.7   Value Chain

CREATING VALUE CHAINS

The creation of value chains allows a firm to better understand the linkages between IC and corporate value: which IC management activities are most associated with its corporate value and which activities are worthy of additional management attention.

Step One: Identifying the Key IC Value Desired

Like many IC activities, the creation of a value chain begins with a review of the corporate vision, its strategy, and the roles for its intellectual capital. Using this information, the firm may consider all of the ways its IC could or should bring value.

The firm should create a list of the kinds of value it wishes to realize from its IC, in order of importance. The relative priority assigned to these values must be continually reviewed and monitored, because priorities can and do change!

Step Two: Determining How to Measure the Value

This step is perhaps the most important; it is certainly the most difficult and the most frequently neglected one. Its purpose is to define *exactly* what value the firm wishes to realize through its IC; this means determining how each specified value will be measured. For example, if a firm believes that the major value of its IC is in its customer relationships, it needs to decide how to measure that value qualitatively or quantitatively.

Step Three: Determining the Value Chain Activities

Using the IAM system as a basis, identify the transitions, activities, and decisions that occur between the development of an innovative idea and the value determined in Step One. These activities should be carefully selected to produce the value in measurable terms, as defined by Step Two.

Step Four: Developing Measures for Managing the Value Chain Activities

Once the IC management activities are defined in the value chain, managers need to ensure that they are managed effectively. In this step the firm develops measures of both process and output for the key activities to ensure that the firm delivers the value from its IC that was defined in Step One. (For a discussion of how to develop measures of IC activity, see the Appendix.)

Step Five: Allocating the Firm's Resources to Maximize IC Value

Resources (e.g., people, dollars, and management attention) should be allocated across the firm according to guidelines that are based on a set of common-sense priorities, such as the following:

- Value-added activities (both value creation and value extraction) should receive resources on a first-priority basis. If sufficient resources are available, then value-added activities should be fully funded. If resources are scarce, then value-added activities should be better funded than either direct-support or indirect-support activities.

- After an evaluation of the company's relative strengths and its relative needs for value creation and value extraction, resources should be allocated or reallocated to ensure that activities most important to the firm's strategy are either fully funded or better funded than others.

- Resource allocation should be weighted toward those activities that are most important to obtaining the value selected by the CEO and those that are most frequently required in the management of the firm's IC.

ALLOCATING INTERNAL INVESTMENT RESOURCES

Every CEO wants to get the greatest return (profit) from the firm's resources and expenditures. The asset allocation question facing the CEO is not dissimilar from the asset allocation investment decision facing individual investors. In researching investor success, a 1986 study of 91 large U.S. pension plans over a ten-year period revealed that *investment policy* explained 93.6 percent of variation in total return.[1] Investment policy, as used in this study, means the allocation of invested assets into different kinds of alternative investments (e.g., stocks, bonds, sectors, and relative weights). The implications of this finding are potentially significant for knowledge companies who must allocate their own assets between tangibles and intangibles. What portion of the company's resources are best placed where? Should more resources be allocated to research? To the licensing office? To human resources? And by what set of standards does the CEO make such decisions?

All of these investment and resource allocation decisions are facilitated by using the IC perspective. The IC framework suggests that a CEO should ask the following questions: How and where does my company add value for our customers? Are the company's resources commensurately allocated to the activities that create the value we provide to our customers?

From the perspective of value extraction, an IC manager might well ask the same sorts of questions as the CEO, but at the organizational level. For example: Which of the company's IC activities are more important than others from the value creation/value extraction perspective? Do the company's resource allocations reflect this relative importance?

To answer questions such as the foregoing, it is helpful to explore three areas of focus for the company:

1. The kinds of value the company wishes to extract from its IC
2. The relative importance of each IC management activity to obtaining the desired value
3. The need or requirement for each IC activity in the course of extracting the desired kind of value.

THE RELATIVE IMPORTANCE OF IC ACTIVITIES

Earlier chapters discussed how a company determines what kind of value to extract from its intellectual capital. The second issue above, how to determine the relative importance of each IC management activity, involves determining the relative importance of value creation and value extraction as well as identifying the specific activities that are most important to the firm's quest to obtain certain kinds of value from its IC.

What Are the Company's Value-Added Activities?

Some companies add value in the form of the products they provide to customers. Other companies add value through relationships and still others add value through their ability to provide their product or service at lower prices than the competition. It is up to each company to determine exactly what it does to add value.

What Is the Source of the Value Added by the Company?

The source of value may be located anywhere in the firm. Although most firms think they know the source of the value they provide for their customers, many have never examined the issue in much detail. Indeed, there are several questions on this topic:

- How are the company's resources allocated? To unique assets? To differentiated assets? To generic assets? What percentage of each?
- Where does the company create value? In unique assets? In differentiated assets? In generic assets? What percentage of each?
- How should the company create value in the future?
- How should the company's resources be allocated? To unique assets? To differentiated assets? To generic assets? What percentage of each?

The Relative Frequency of Requirement for IC Activities

The intellectual asset management system can be used to determine the activities associated with extracting any kind of value. Exhibits 4.3 through 4.7 provide us with examples of these activities. But if a manufacturing firm wanted to learn which portions of the IAMS were used most frequently (as one measure of their importance in making resource allocation decisions), it could compile the information in a form similar to that shown in Exhibit 4.8.

From the information displayed in Exhibit 4.8 we can see that a manufacturing company needs the ability to perform the following IC activities:

- Innovation
- Decision-making about whether to obtain legal protection for its innovations
- Securing legal protection for selected innovations
- Developing a portfolio database
- Valuation
- Evaluation of innovations in the context of the firm's business strategy, market tactics, and competitive environment
- Decision-making about how to dispose of the innovation, how to extract strategic positioning value, and how to extract cash flow value

SUMMARY

The process of value extraction begins with a definition of the company's vision for itself and its strategy for achieving the vision. Determining the roles intellectual capital may play in achieving the vision and enabling the strategy is a key step to identifying the specific kinds of value to be extracted from the IC. But realizing the specified value requires several important steps. First, the specified value must be defined in ways that make it measurable. Next, the firm must think through what it needs to accomplish in order to realize each specified kind of value. This latter process is helped by creating value chains that describe and define the activities, decisions, and work processes that are required. The value chains then highlight what activities the firm must be involved with, what must be managed, and which activity is important to measure. The value chains also highlight where management must focus the

Exhibit 4.8   An IC Value Chain Matrix

Kind of Value	Source of IC	Protection	Portfolio Database	Valuation	Evaluation	Disposition Decision	Value Extraction Decision	Final Action
Product & Service Sales	Innovation	Protection (Yes/No) → Obtain Protection	Patent Portfolio Database	Valuation	Evaluate vis-à-vis Business Strategies	Disposition Decision	Commercialization Decision	Sell
Trademark	Innovation	Protection (Yes/No) → Obtain Protection	Trademark Portfolio Database	Valuation	Evaluate vis-à-vis Business Strategies	Disposition Decision	Commercialization Decision; Strategic Positioning	Promote Trademark; Set Premium Price
Name Recognition	Innovation	Protection (Yes/No) → Obtain Protection	Trademark Portfolio Database	Valuation	Evaluate vis-à-vis Business Strategies	Disposition Decision	Strategic Positioning	Implement Plan; Monitor/Measure Results
Relationships	Relationships with Customers			Valuation	Evaluate vis-à-vis Business Strategies	Disposition Decision	Strategic Positioning	Implement Plan; Measure and Monitor Results

firm's energies in order to maximize the value to be extracted from its intellectual capital.

NOTE

1. Brinson, G., L. R. Hood, and G. Beebower, "Determinants of Portfolio Performance," *Financial Analysts Journal,* July–August, 1986, pp. 39–44.

Part II

Valuing Knowledge Companies

5

Valuing Knowledge Companies (Basic Concepts)

In earlier chapters we defined and discussed intellectual capital, the IC framework, and its three dimensions, as well as the kinds of value that intellectual capital brings to a corporation. We have discussed value in terms of its direct or indirect nature and offensive or defensive nature. All of these discussions were important in understanding intellectual capital and the IC framework.

With the foregoing well established we can turn our attention to a question that is foremost in the minds of many: a discussion of value in terms of its *amount*. Many will argue that this may be the most important topic for a book such as this. Indeed, to any reader involved with commercial companies or business activity, the question of "how much is it worth?" is of fundamental interest and importance. Discussion of "how much" has been withheld until this point because most people look for the answer in an accounting context. As we have learned, we have to look to a different system to determine the *amount* of value of a firm's intellectual capital.

THE RELATIONSHIP BETWEEN IC
AND THE DOLLAR VALUE OF A FIRM

There are many skeptics when it comes to determining the amount of value of a firm's intangible assets. This is often frustrating to the IC faithful. Whereas the faithful will subscribe to fuzzy or imprecise measures of value, the skeptics often want to see "cash on the barrel head"! As we learned earlier, one of the difficulties with determining IC value is that a large portion of the value is indirect. Since indirect value (e.g., strategic positioning, reputation, image) is difficult to quantify in dollar terms, it is difficult to put into a form that satisfies the skeptics. Also, it is sometimes difficult to know what people in an organization consider to be of value. An idea that is held to be of little value in one organization may be of great value in another because the two organizations value different things. This chapter is about the concepts that underlie determining the *amount* of value that intellectual capital has for an organization. In Chapters 6 and 7 we will discuss how to perform calculations to quantify the amount. Here we will lay some necessary groundwork.

To briefly review, we know that intellectual capital is important because it creates the future products and services of the firm; the firm's future cash flows. We also know that a firm's dollar value is the sum of two of its financial parts: the dollar value of its tangible assets and the present value of its future cash flows. If this is true then it follows that IC is linked to the dollar value of a firm! The degree to which IC links to future revenues is the degree to which it has an impact on the firm's dollar value; and on its market value (or stock price)!

We know that the stock market values companies, in large part, by their ability to produce revenue, cash flow, and profits; so the degree to which IC is an integral part of creating these elements is the degree to which it impacts the dollar value of the firm and its stock price.

Having established the importance of IC to the firm's future revenues, cash flows, and profits and thereby to the firm's value and stock price, we now turn to a discussion of value, and how it is determined.

WHAT IS VALUE?

Value is a concept with many interpretations. Which of these interpretations applies to an organization or business depends, of course, on the beholder. Value as discussed in this book will be from the perspective of the economist. To people with this view, value is related to usefulness.

Nothing can have value without being an object of utility. If it be useless, the labor contained in it is useless, cannot be reckoned as labor, and cannot therefore create value.[1]

Value is different from cost, as it is also different from price. Value is a measure of the usefulness of something, whereas cost is a measure of the amount of resources required to produce it. Price, by way of further contrast, measures what an item's owner believes others will pay for it.

Value is the life-giving power of anything; cost, the quantity of labor required to produce it; price, the quantity of labor which its possessor will take in exchange for it.[2]

A cynic is a man who knows the price of everything, and the value of nothing.[3]

Value is relative. For example, the value of a piece of rental property may be assessed differently by a seller, a potential buyer, an insurance company, a tax assessor, the executor of an estate containing the property, a government entity considering taking possession by "eminent domain," or a potential mortgage lender. The value assigned to an item depends primarily on the needs of the person or organization seeking to quantify the value.

In the business context, value measurements are used for decision making. The value of an intangible or a piece of intellectual capital is often the basis for deciding whether to invest further in developing the intangible, to continue holding it, or to sell it. This kind of value measurement may be called economic.

To the economist, "value" is a measure of the utility that ownership of an item brings to its owner. Utility is often viewed as a stream of benefits, stretching into the future, that an owner foresees as the "rent" received from owning the item. Utility may be measured in a number of ways. To the visual artist, utility may be the pleasure the work gives to the viewer. To the designer, utility may be the functionality of a design. To the accountant, utility may be measured in the accuracy of historical expenditure data. To the economist, however, utility is most often measured in dollar terms.

Economists typically view a future stream of benefits in dollar terms and can discount and sum these amounts to determine the current dollar equivalent of a future stream of income. This discounting and summing calculation is the determination of the net present value of a future stream of benefits. This is most often the economist's measure of value.

Looked at through economic eyes, the value associated with a knowledge firm lies largely in the knowledge it creates for future commercialization as well as the capabilities it creates to extract current profits from existing knowledge.

There are real differences between accountants, economists, and IC practitioners about how to value intellectual capital. These differences are significant and reflect, on the one hand, a growing awareness of the difficulty with using traditional accounting to measure the value of intellectual assets; and, on the other hand, a common interest in developing better and more useful measurement tools. Among the most innovative thinking about new methods for measuring intangibles, beyond those found in traditional accounting, is being spear-headed by the Canadian Board of Chartered Accountants.

WHAT AFFECTS VALUE?

In the case of intangibles, such as intellectual capital, value is largely dependent on the firm's view of itself and on the realities of its marketplace. Put another way, each firm exists within a context that shapes its view of what is or is not of value. Context may be defined as the firm's internal and external realities.

Questions asked to determine the internal dimensions of context center on direction, resources, and constraints. What business is the firm really in? How does the firm define its business? What are the firm's strengths and weaknesses? What are the levers to pull for growth? What strategies are available? What strategies has the firm selected? Why? What is the firm's current performance against goal? Is this performance acceptable? What are the political realities of the firm? What is politically correct thinking within the firm and what is not? What is "do-able"?

Questions asked to determine the external context center on identifying the fundamental forces affecting the industry as well as the immediate opportunities available in the firm's marketplace. What are the major environmental forces affecting success in this business (e.g., economic, governmental, technological, sociological, political)? What is the firm's market? How is it changing (getting larger, declining, etc.)? Who are the firm's competitors? What are their strengths and weaknesses? What are the best market strategies?

We have all had the experience of initiating an idea that was subsequently minimized or abandoned by the organization, despite its apparent initial value, only to learn later that another company had successfully implemented something quite similar. A good idea that could not grow in one context took root and flourished in another. Context is important!

The Importance of Values and Vision

Companies that successfully manage their intellectual capital realize that *values* and *vision* are fundamental to determining what a firm believes to have value. A firm's values are major determinants of what it holds to be of value.[4] Once the firm's values are known, it becomes possible to know how a firm should value an item. The importance of vision (already discussed as a part of the IC framework) is based on similar but different reasoning. If a firm has a vision of what it wants to become, then it will be able to know whether an item (of intellectual capital) will help move the company toward that vision. If an item would be helpful, then it has value for the firm. If it has no usefulness in moving the firm toward its vision or objectives, then it has little value.

Vision

A firm's vision describes the company as it wishes to be in the future. The vision often provides the standard against which a new innovation is measured: Will the innovation help the firm achieve its long-term vision? Can the firm capitalize on or somehow use the innovation to improve internal operations, how it is viewed by the marketplace? Will it lead to increased sales? Will it improve internal efficiency? Will it improve the firm's ability to develop new innovations? Are these things important to the firm? If so, the idea has value. If not, then the idea has little value.

Values

The values of a firm represent the consensus beliefs of an organization's members. The sum of these views, the collective values of the firm, determine the worldview held by the employees. Values drive the employees' day-to-day decision making and if their values differ from those of the executive management, the employees will be unlikely to implement the firm's strategic plan effectively. Values may be thought of as ideals that shape and give significance to our lives. They are reflected in the priorities we choose, the decisions we make, and the actions we take. Values are ideals that individuals select and use as the basis for many decisions in day-to-day life. As decision prioritizers, values are reflected in behavior. As ideals, they provide meaning for people's lives. Values are also measurable. They represent the lens through which individuals and organizations view the world. An item has value (i.e., worth) to an organization if it is consistent with its values. Items that are *not* consistent with a firm's values have little value to the firm.

Values set the context within which a firm may determine what it holds to be of value (or worth). Vision sets the benchmark against which corporations may *measure* the value of their intangibles.

TIME

A *current time* versus *future time* dimension, associated with intellectual capital, is most apparent in companies, such as product companies, where the intellectual capital is involved in an R&D activity. For these companies, intellectual properties may be thought of as the source of current value for the firm. Much of what is currently in the firm's patent portfolio is the basis for protecting current products in the marketplace or for current joint ventures and strategic alliances. Intellectual properties represent current value where the value extraction activities are rife with tactical considerations. Intellectual assets, the next "tier" of intellectual capital, are the assets with less current definition, and often more promise for the future. Extracting value from these assets usually involves thinking into the future, and discussing positioning and strategies for value extraction rather than near-term tactics. For this reason, intellectual assets are usually considered as assets that bridge the transition from the present to the future (also from the tactical to the strategic) value extraction. The intellectual capital tier operates almost entirely at the strategic level of decision-making and future value extraction, but uses the same fundamental decision processes as those found in the most fundamental and well-constructed systems for extracting value from intellectual property.

For service companies there is a time dimension associated with value, although the tiering of intellectual capital, so obvious in product companies, is much less significant. Service innovations conceived and implemented in the past have already exerted an influence on the firm's cash flow. They have already been incorporated into the firm's offerings, provided to clients, billed, and produced cash revenues. The cash flow from these past innovations has already been booked and is reflected on the firm's financial reports. The current investment in the salaries of the service firm's intellectual capital is expected to produce current sales as well as new innovations or ideas that can be implemented in the immediate future.

ONE-TIME VERSUS ONGOING VALUE

Intellectual capital may be the source for either one-time transaction value or ongoing, cash-flow-producing value. Although the value extraction processes discussed extensively throughout this book relate to the ongoing cash-producing value of intellectual capital, it must be recognized that IC assets are often sold individually or as packaged bundles of intellectual assets.

One-time value could be realized by a sale. This value holds true for the market conditions existing at the time of the sale, while anyone measuring the ongoing value of a going concern values the ability of that operation to continue its business functions on the day after the valuation in much the same way they were conducted the days before. There is clearly defined value in the capacity to continue churning out the products or services that generate the income sought by the purchaser of the knowledge firm under examination. This value distinguishes the going concern from a start-up with a much smaller storehouse of knowledge and learning and less ability to demonstrate broad capabilities for designing, manufacturing, and delivering products to customers.

Going concern value, for a knowledge company, is largely composed of the value of the tacit knowledge of the workforce carrying out the operational functions of the business, thereby making it a going concern. Astute analysts today will seek more understanding of the elements underpinning company operations and "going concern-ness" than would their counterparts decades ago, when going concern value was set at a number that felt good under the circumstances. Often it was based on a finger-in-the-wind estimate thought to be justifiable in the sense that it would pass the "red face" test on presentation to the tax authorities or the financial community. Though it may be no easier today to ascribe a quantifiable valuation, simply understanding what underlies the recognizable value of being a going concern allows a more critical analysis of whether a purchase premium for going concern-ness is in the right order of magnitude.

What is the going concern value of a service company whose tacit knowledge could leave the company shortly after the company is purchased? What is the going concern value of a company producing a product having an unrefreshed life cycle measured in terms of a few months or years (at most) if the tacit knowledge necessary for continuous improvement departs post valuation? When service companies are the focus of a valuation, the fleeting value of tacit knowledge must be a concern. Service firms that are able to convert their employees' tacit knowledge into codified knowledge (intellectual assets) have a greater going concern value than those who do not.

The value of a firm as a going concern may be thought of as having two parts: the value of the tangible assets (typically a relatively small number) and the present value of the firm's cash flow (typically a relatively large number).

- *Tangible asset value* is generally agreed to be calculated (for each tangible asset) as the lesser of either the asset's original cost or its current market value.
- *Cash flow value*, the present value of the firm's future stream of cash flows, is determined in three steps:
  1. The annual cash flows are forecasted.
  2. The cash flows for each year into the future are discounted (to account for the degree of uncertainty that the markets feel exists that the forecasted amount of cash flow will actually materialize.)
  3. The discounted cash flows are summed into a figure that represents the present value of the firm's discounted future cash flows. This term is usually called the net present value (NPV) of the firm's cash flows.

WHY THE DIFFICULTY IN VALUING IC?

From the perspective of the value extractor, intellectual capital brings value to the corporation in two ways: strategic position and financial/economic value. Strategic position is often thought of in qualitative terms (image, competitive posture). Financial or economic value of intellectual capital, on the other hand, is most often thought of in terms that are easy to quantify (price, share, cash flow).

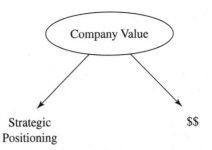

Exhibit 5.1   The Two Kinds of Value Associated with IC

The two different kinds of value measurement associated with intellectual capital, qualitative and quantitative, become apparent when company value is seen in the two dimensions suggested in Exhibit 5.1. In this context we can explore the currently available valuation frameworks to learn how well they can be used to describe qualitative as well as quantitative value.

FRAMEWORKS FOR DETERMINING QUALITATIVE VALUE

There are currently two perspectives from which intellectual capital is qualitatively valued, based on two general views of intellectual capital.

1. *The Knowledge/Knowledge Management Perspective.* This view (oversimplified here) is largely held by people interested in the value creation activities of intellectual capital management. It holds that the creation of new business-related knowledge or the sharing of existing knowledge within the firm are fundamentally desirable activities. The degree to which new knowledge is created or to which knowledge may be more widely shared determines the value of an activity or asset.

When Xerox established its new research facility in Palo Alto, California in the 1970s, it instructed the director to hire the brightest people and to allow them to pursue interesting ideas. This approach to creating a research facility was consistent with a Knowledge/Knowledge Management perspective. Indeed, when asked whether the facility should instead focus on hiring people with knowledge about paper, printing, and xerography, the Xerox top management said they wanted their research unit to be as broadly creative as possible. Their reasoning was that with all of that creativity, some of it just had to prove valuable to Xerox.

2. *The Value Extraction Perspective.* This view holds that the degree to which an item of intellectual capital aids the firm in moving toward its strategic vision or better enables the firm to operationalize its strategy, is a measure of its qualitative value. To illustrate, the staff that Xerox hired for its research facility actually invented and produced (in the 1970s) the first of what were later to be called personal computers. The research staff approached Xerox management seeking to commercialize this revolutionary new product. The very management who had established the research unit with a magnanimous knowledge/knowledge management philosophy was now forced to realize that the company had no capability to produce, market, and service this new and distinctly different kind of product. After all, they came to realize, Xerox was then a company making its profits selling copier paper and toner. They knew a lot about how to manufacture and sell copier paper and toner and nothing at all about how to manufacture, sell, and service personal computers. Although the company took an enormous amount of criticism for not pursuing the personal computer, their lack of the complementary business assets required to commercialize this innovative product

meant that their decision saved the company from investing (and probably losing) significant amounts of capital in a business they knew nothing about.

FRAMEWORKS FOR QUANTIFYING VALUE

The nature of business as well as the history of its evolution is such that the art of *quantifying* value is further advanced than that of determining its *qualitative* value. When it comes to quantifying value, a number of paradigms and quantification systems may be used, for example:

- Accounting (asset-based and cash flow-based valuations)
- Economics (economic rents and contributions of capitals)
- Intellectual capital
- Shareholder value

Similarly, there are a number of conditions under which firms may be valued:

- Going concern value
- Stock market value
- Mergers and acquisitions (M&A) value

MEASURING INTELLECTUAL CAPITAL

When the firm's intellectual capital is aligned with its vision and strategy, the roles for IC may become known, and their value measurable. IC roles are typically divided into two sets: value creation and value extraction. The subdivision into these two, and further subdivisions as desired, make it easier to determine the components of value to be measured.

Once the "what" of IC measurement is known, it is necessary to decide *how* to measure it. Here it is useful to differentiate between measures and measurements as follows:

- *Measures*—the dimensions to be used in the act of measuring.
- *Measuring*—the act of comparing the thing to be measured against the standard dimensions proscribed.
- *Measurements*—the numerical results of measuring.

Quantitative vs. Qualitative Measures of Value

Measures may be either qualitative or quantitative. Qualitative measures are typically judgement-based and often are used when the item to be measured or the attribute of interest does not lend itself to precise or quantifiable measurement. One of the most striking examples of this phenomena may be best exemplified by using a non-business intangible: love. Parents are often asked by their child, "How much do you love me?" The answer, of course, defies quantification. As respondents to that question parents tend to fall back on answers like: "A lot!"

The point is that some things, even very important ones like love, do not lend themselves to accurate or quantifiable measurement. Sometimes, when it is difficult to measure an IC activity directly, companies have found that they can use indicators rather than measures. Because direct measurement often requires that something be completed before it can be counted, there are times when we need to measure work-in-progress. Indicators are helpful under these circumstances because they are less definitive than measures. Although they also provide information on amount, they are often fuzzy, using terms like "a lot" or "more than." Indicators are often defined in terms that are not as black-and-white as normal quantitative measures. This means that companies can define measures that are gray instead of only those that are black and white.

Vectors are another form of measurement that works well when measuring intellectual capital activities. Vectors are helpful because they provide information on direction as well as on amount. A vector measurement might be that the company's intellectual capital has "increased substantially" over the past year, meaning that the vector of change is positive in direction and the length of the vector is relatively long. On the other hand, some companies might find that their intellectual capital had "decreased somewhat" as a result of an early retirement policy. This represents a vector that points in a downward direction, and one whose length is relatively short.

Quantitative measures may be integer- or vector-based. For the integer-based measures, there are two further divisions: financial or non-financial. Exhibit 5.2 highlights sample measures under each heading.

When most of us think of measurement, we immediately think of quantitative measures such as feet, time, weight, dollars, and so on. These measures allow us to determine where we have been, where we are going (in terms of distance and time), and where we are today in a physical sense. For companies, in the past largely concerned with physical assets, measurement has traditionally centered around quantitative outputs—in particular amounts of product, dollars, and sometimes time. Quantitative measures provide a precise snapshot of the firm's activities and in doing so, quantitative measurement requires that there be points at which measurement may be taken. In other words, quantitative measurement requires discreet measurements which are very useful to tell us what *has* happened.

Qualitative measures give us a sense of what *is* happening. They are useful for telling us the vector of change rather than the speed and are useful for answering questions such as "Is the amount of your firm's intellectual capital changing?" The answer to such a question might include the direction (up or down) and the general degree of change (a lot, a little, a moderate amount). Qualitative measures are often most useful when

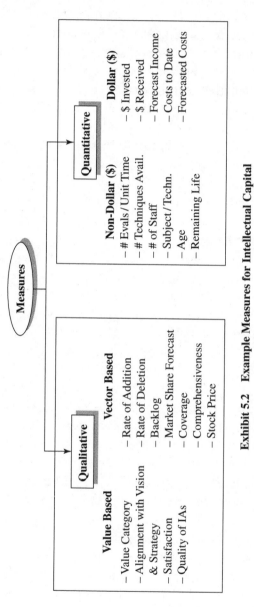

Exhibit 5.2 Example Measures for Intellectual Capital

Source: Patrick H. Sullivan, *Profiting from Intellectual Capital: Extracting Value from Innovation.* Copyright © 1998 by John Wiley & Sons, Inc. Reprinted by permission of John Wiley & Sons, Inc.

put into the context of the firm. For example, in a survey of portfolio managers who were asked to define their patent portfolio, managers responded in the following terms:

- The technologies included
- Strategic objectives and intent for the portfolio
- Strategic use of the portfolio
- Value of the portfolio (both qualitative and quantitative)
- Income and cost associated with the portfolio

With the exception of the final category, all of the other dimensions the portfolio managers used to define and describe this set of intellectual assets (a patent portfolio) are qualitative.

NOTES

1. *Capital* (1867–1883), pt. II, ch. 3.
2. *Munera Pulveris* (1862), ch. 1.
3. *Lady Windemere's Fan* (1892), Act III, Scene 2.
4. B. Hall, "Culture and Values Management," from P. Sullivan's *Profiting from Intellectual Capital*, John Wiley & Sons, 1998.

6

Valuing Knowledge Companies for Merger or Acquisition

INTRODUCTION

The myriad of small start-up companies seen in recent years include many whose major value lies with their intellectual capital. For these companies their worth resides in both their existing innovations and their ability to generate more. In contrast, larger firms in many industries are learning that while there are many advantages to size, it often has an inhibiting effect on innovation. One way such firms have learned to obtain access to new and creative thinking is to acquire the small firms whose value lies with their innovative capabilities. These firms, sometimes called boutiques, are filled with creative ideas and innovations (intellectual capital) yet often lack sufficient working capital or cash (structural capital) to survive and flourish. For the large firm, acquiring small firms such as these provides access to the innovation and energy they seek while the owner-innovators in the small firm are provided with an opportunity to cash out (get paid for their stock of intellectual capital) as well as for continued employment, including a guaranteed salary, for doing something they enjoy.

The difficulty in valuing knowledge companies (such as these boutiques) for mergers or acquisition is that the state of the art for valuing intangible assets is still in its infancy. There is not yet a generally accepted set of methods for valuing intangible assets to the degree of precision desired. In addition, as discussed in Chapter 5, valuing a company depends very much on the context of the company and the reason for which it is being valued. Valuing one company for acquisition by another is very different from valuing a company as a going concern. In the latter case, typically the way in which the stock market considers value, a valuation would consider the long-term cash flow generation capability of the firm and discount that back to present value. The DCF (discounted cash flow) plus the market value of the firm's tangible assets represent the major elements that define the value of the going concern. In the former case, valuing a company for merger or acquisition, the value of the firm depends more on what it can add to the acquiring firm's value than what it can generate in terms of cash on its own. To make matters worse, the accounting discipline is not helpful when it comes to intangible assets. Accounting is a transaction-based discipline, relying on market transactions for valuing assets. In the case of intangibles there is often no transaction available, hence accounting's helplessness in valuing companies having a large portion of their value associated with innovations or with the innovative capabilities of their employees.

This chapter discusses an IC-based method for valuing knowledge companies for merger or acquisition. The method is not intended for valuing companies under other circumstances. Its main focus is to determine how much value an intellectual capital company may bring to an acquirer and how to determine how much of that value could reasonably be paid to the acquired company and how much should be retained by the acquiring company.

THE IMPORTANCE OF COMPLEMENTARY BUSINESS ASSETS

In a merger or acquisition context, the interest of the purchasing company (let's call it Acme Widget) is in some particular portion of the intellectual capital of the company to be acquired (let's call it Beautific Baubles.) We can say that Acme Widget is interested in that portion of Beautific Baubles' intellectual assets which, when matched with Acme's complementary business assets, should produce a particularly high return. In addition, Acme may see something in Beautific's complementary business assets that could provide extra value to Acme. All other Beautific intellectual capital and complementary business assets objectively should not be of much interest to Acme and typically should be viewed as having little retention value except for the cash that might be available through a sell-off of unwanted assets.

In this case, note that Acme Widget is primarily interested in a portion of Beautific Baubles' intellectual capital because, by applying Beautific's IC to the complementary business assets of Acme, the amount of value that can be created is significantly more than Beautific could ever have created using its (typically) less extensive complementary business assets.

For the purpose of describing the new entity that emerges from the acquisition/merger of the two companies (Acme and Beautific) there is a new organization, which we may call Newco. You will recall the equation for the value of a going-concern company, where the value was equal to the sum of the value of the company's tangible assets and its discounted cash flow. Therefore, the value of Newco may be expressed in equation form as follows:

$$Vnewco = V(TA) + DCF$$

However, if one company (Company A) acquires another (Company B), the formula is slightly modified. The new equation is also quite simple. It says that the value of Newco is the sum of all of Company A's and Company B's tangible assets and discounted cash flows. So, the value of Newco's tangible assets is the sum of the tangible assets of both firms:

$$\text{Tangible assets of Newco} = TA_A + TA_B$$

And the cash flows of Newco are the sum of four combinations from companies A and B:

1. The IC of Company A and the complementary business assets of Company A.
2. The IC of Company A and the complementary business assets of Company B.
3. The IC of Company B and the complementary business assets of Company A.
4. The IC of Company B and the complementary business assets of Company B.

$$
\begin{aligned}
\text{Vnewco} &= V_{TA} + V_{DCF} \\
&= [VTA_A + VTA_B] + [f(V(IC)_A, CBA_A) + \\
&\quad f(V(IC)_A, CBA_B) + f(V(IC)_B + CBA_A) + \\
&\quad f(V(IC)_B + CBA_B)]
\end{aligned}
$$

There is something very interesting about the four cash flow terms (combinations from companies A and B) in the valuation equation. Several of these terms may not be important to the value of Newco and may even be ignored. For example, if Company A acquired Company B largely because of Company B's intellectual capital then we can simplify the valuation calculation significantly. For example:

1. The value of the first combination, Company A's IC and Company A's complementary business assets (or, the value

of Company A as a going-concern) is already known and need not be recalculated.

2. The value of the IC of Company A and the complementary business assets of Company B is of no interest. Company A did not acquire Company B for its complementary assets. Indeed, they probably hold little value for Company A. This term may be ignored.

3. The IC of Company B and the complementary business assets of Company A is the key term in this valuation equation. To determine the value of this term, we must identify the particular pieces of Company B's intellectual capital of interest, the kind of cash value desired, the value chain for developing this value, and the activities involved.

4. The final combination term, the IC of Company B and the complementary assets of Company B, is probably not of interest because in our scenario Company A purchased Company B in order to match up the IC of B with Company A's complementary business assets. Company B's complementary business assets are probably of no interest. If so, final combination term can be ignored. (If, for any reason, this term is of interest, the value of Company B's IC when matched to B's complementary business assets represents the value of Company B as a going concern. This value is already known.)

As the result of the foregoing, the actual equation for the value of Newco looks like:

$$\mathbf{Vnewco} = [\mathbf{VTA_A} + \mathbf{VTA_B}] + [\mathbf{f(\,V(IC)_A,\ CBA_A\,)} + f(\,V(IC)A,\ CBAB) + \mathbf{f(\,V(IC)_B,\ CBA_A\,)} + f(\,V(IC)B,\ CBAB)]$$

In calculating the value of the new enterprise, the most important terms in the valuation equation are the value of the tangible assets, the value of Company A as a going concern, and the incremental value realized by combining the IC of Company B with the complementary business assets of Company A. The financial analyst making such calculations will find that the value of the tangible assets is known (it is already on the balance sheets of the two firms), and the value of Company A as a going concern is known. The only portion of the value to be calculated is the value of the IC of Company B and the complementary business assets of Company A.

DEFINING THE PURCHASE PRICE
USING THE IC PERSPECTIVE

The amount of dollar value produced by combining the IC of Company B with the complementary business assets of Company A represents the new dollar value made possible by the combination of the two companies. Part of this dollar value represents the value brought by Company B and the remainder represents the value brought by Company A. The amount of this value that goes to Company B as its purchase price should reflect the portion of the newly created value that is associated with its IC. Similarly the portion of the value that is associated with the complementary business assets of Company A should remain with Company A and not be included in the purchase price for B.

CALCULATING THE PURCHASE PRICE
USING THE IC PERSPECTIVE

The calculation of a purchase price requires that the parties understand how the intellectual assets of the acquired company will bring value to the acquiring company. The acquired company needs to understand how much value its intellectual assets will create for the acquirer in order to estimate how much it (the acquired company) should receive in compensation. Likewise, the company making the acquisition needs to understand fully what value the acquired intellectual assets will bring and can then determine how much it is willing to spend to obtain them.

Determining the purchase price involves several steps on the part of the acquiring company:

1. Definition of assets of interest for acquisition
2. How acquired assets are expected to be used
3. Determination of amount of value created by acquired assets
4. Determination of purchase price for acquired assets

The steps involved in calculating the purchase price are detailed in the following descriptions:

Step One: Definition of Assets of Interest for Acquisition

The acquiring company needs to determine what about the target company it wishes to possess: What are the assets of interest? Are they intellectual assets? If so, which ones? Are they the human capital? Particular individuals whose knowledge or know-how is deemed particularly valuable? Are any of the structural capital assets of interest? Which ones? Why? How would they be integrated into the acquiring company's capital assets?

Step Two: How Acquired Assets are Expected to Be Used

The acquiring company must determine how these assets would be used: Would they leverage existing complementary assets? Would they leverage existing intellectual assets? Would they shorten time to market? Would they help gain access to future technology? Markets? Position?

Step Three: Determination of Amount of Value Created by Acquired Assets

The acquiring company must calculate the additional value that would be created by using the acquired assets:

1. List the intellectual assets of Firm A subject to the acquisition. For each, identify their intended use by Firm B.

   The acquiring company, Firm B, is in most cases interested in the company to be acquired because of one or more items of intellectual capital owned by Firm A. Most often, it is the set of intellectual capital items that Firm B in particular wishes to acquire. Firm B's reasoning is that those pieces of intellectual capital, when combined with Firm B's complementary business assets, could produce a significant increase in revenue or profits for Firm B. In order for this to be the case, Firm B should have some a priori understanding of which specific intellectual assets of Firm A it wishes to acquire and, for each, what it would do with them if they were acquired. To begin the process of determining the value of the selected pieces of intellectual capital, Firm B must list them and, for each, describe how they intend to use them in their business or operations. This should include the intended conversion mechanisms.

2. For each intellectual asset, describe the intellectual asset management activities concerned with its use.

   Part of Firm B's ability to extract value from the intellectual capital it wishes to acquire from Firm A is Firm B's ability to successfully determine how to integrate each piece of intellectual capital into its business operations. The capability for such an evaluation is part of Firm B's Intellectual Asset Management System (IAMS). Firm B should list the activities and decisions required of the IAMS in determining the manner and means for extracting the desired value from its acquired intellectual capital.

3. For each intellectual asset, identify and describe the Complementary Business Assets (CBAs) to be used.

   The identification and description of the CBAs should include a preliminary calculation of the new costs expected to be incurred by the operation of the CBA.

4. Define the chain of activities associated with creating the value that emerges from the intended use.

   The chain of activities should consist of an identification of the activities involved and, for each, the preliminary calculation of marginal costs expected to be incurred for each piece of intellectual capital processed.

Step Four: Determination of Purchase Price for Acquired Assets

Both the acquiring and the target company need to determine an acceptable purchase price. The purchaser determines the highest price it would be willing to pay to obtain the cash flow calculated in Step 3. The seller determines the least it would be willing to accept in compensation for the income stream.

SUMMARY

This chapter has discussed the quantitative value of knowledge companies in two different kinds of situations: the value as a going concern (the stock market value), and the value in a merger or acquisition scenario. In addition, methods for defining the value of an acquired company, both qualitatively and quantitatively, have been described. Finally a method for determining the price to be paid for the acquisition of a knowledge company has been presented.

7

Linking Intellectual Capital with Stock Price

In recent years the number of companies whose value lies largely with their intellectual capital has increased dramatically. In a study of thousands of non-financial companies over a 20-year period, Dr. Margaret Blair, of the Brookings Institute, reported a significant shift in the makeup of company assets. She studied all of the non-financial publicly traded firms in the Compustat database. In 1978, her study showed that 80 percent of the firms' value was associated with its tangible assets, with 20 percent associated with its intangible assets. In 10 years, by 1988, the makeup had shifted to 45 percent tangible assets and 55 percent intangible assets. By 1998, only 30 percent of the value of the firms studied was attributable to tangible assets while a stunning 70 percent was associated with the value of their intangibles.

This shift of corporate value away from tangible assets and toward intangible assets is consistent with the shift we observe in the United States economy and in the economies of the industrialized west. One can also predict that this shift will continue worldwide as the value of information and innovation continues to grow.

WHY THE SHIFT TOWARD INTANGIBLES?

The reasons for this shift toward a greater portion of corporate value lying with intangible assets are many, and the following are among the major factors:

1. *The Changing Legal Environment.* It can no longer be questioned that the creation of the new Court of Appeals for the Federal Circuit in 1982 has had an immeasurably positive effect on the value of patents, one of the major forms of intangible assets in U.S. firms. The subsequently greater number of decisions in favor of the holder of intellectual property (IP) rights since the court's creation has made patent holder rights more enforceable and therefore possessed of greater value.

In addition, the shift in the perspective of the Supreme Court away from a focus on anti-trust concerns to a view that balances the monopoly rights of patent holders with anti-trust considerations has further tended to enhance the value of IP rights. Finally, within the halls of the U.S. Department of Justice, the lessening of what had previously been an almost maniacal anti-trust stance to one that recognizes, if not encourages, the importance of the monopoly rights of patent holders, has also contributed to the increasing value of IP.

2. *Effects of the Internet and Information Technology.* The rapid rise of the Internet in parallel with the exponentially growing capabilities of information technology (computers, communications, etc.) has effectively moved the industrialized world into a new economic paradigm: the economics of abundance. In the industrial era tangible assets were the major source of value; but, in the information era information has more value than tangible assets.

In the industrial paradigm, companies operated under the tenets of the economics of scarcity. If a company owned a tangible asset, for example, gold, that company possessed the gold and others did not. The company's gold had value as long as gold was a relatively scarce commodity and the company could limit access to it.

In the information age things are quite different. Information, different from tangible assets, increases in value the more people there are who have access to it. The economics of abundance means that when we make information abundant, its value goes up. The implications of the economics of abundance are such that firms may give away for free the things they used to charge for, and charge for a new set of products or services whose value is increased because of the information or intangible that has been provided for free. For example, rock bands could probably afford to provide free tickets to their concerts because the amount of money they make on t-shirts, CD's, and similar follow-on products could be much greater than the income from the concerts themselves. As another example, several web companies found they fared better economically when they provided their browsers for free and charged fees for access to some of the information accessed via the browser.

3. *The Leveraging Effect of Intellectual Capital.* Intellectual capital has the ability to leverage the profitability of the firm. It has allowed firms to create new products and services, new business processes, and new organizational forms. In 1979 a Swedish forest products company, Esselte, came to SRI International because it was concerned with all of the then recent talk of a paperless office. This company, who for over one hundred years had created a series of paper-based products, wanted to know more about how its business was threatened and what it could do to stave off the threat. Although the initial focus of the project was to identify threats, SRI soon demonstrated that Esselte had a significant number of new opportunities that only became apparent when the company's perspective was changed from a paper-based view to an information-based one. It turned out that Esselte owned the company that printed the Swedish

law books. This printing company was located across the street from the Legislature and the law books were printed on computer-controlled presses, meaning that the company had a computer file of all of the country's laws. This presented an opportunity to provide an electronic legal search service for Swedish lawyers. This is just one example of how a company learned to convert a tangible assets business into one based on intangibles: knowledge and information.

As another example of the leveraging effect of intellectual capital, Professor Stanley Davis of Boston University, in his book, *Future Perfect*, predicted that for companies to be successful in the twenty-first century they would have to do several things, one of which was to put more information (intangible value) into their products. For Davis, this meant providing more intelligence in the same amount of product mass, or providing the same amount of intelligence in a smaller amount of product mass. Over the course of the past few years we have seen Davis's prediction come true. Consider the automobile. At the end of the twentieth century, cars are one of the major users of computer chips. There are computers that operate the engine more efficiently, computers that shift gears, computers in our car telephones, computers that navigate our cars using the global positioning system. Finally there are computers that turn our windshield wipers or automobile lights on and off. Cars are not noticeably bigger or smaller but the amount of information contained in them has increased dramatically in the last decade.

Also, consider other products that contain more and more information or intangible value per unit of volume: telephones, computers, appliances, childrens' toys, credit cards with embedded chips, bar codes on retail products, office copiers that self-diagnose their own operating problems; the list is endless. All of these products or services are possible because they build upon the innovations of the intellectual capital of their producers.

DETERMINING THE VALUE
OF A KNOWLEDGE COMPANY

There is a diverse audience of people interested in learning how to determine the value of a knowledge company. The CEO of the firm is interested in this topic. If he does not provide investors with a continuing return on their investment he is at risk of being voted out at the next shareholders' meeting. Chief financial officers, as the internal surrogates to the CEO for financial matters, are also likely to find this topic of great interest. Outside of the firm, there are interested parties in government regulatory agencies, in business research centers, and in academia. Surprisingly, there is little interest in this topic from the financial analyst community, a group one would think would find this topic of great interest. At a recent meeting of the ICM Gathering devoted to a discussion of the relationship between IC and stock price, very few financial analysts expressed any interest in this topic at all. Fewer still would devote time to attend a meeting to discuss it, and when the discussion took place, we learned that most of the few analysts attending viewed companies through an accounting perspective and believed that their forecasts of future income (based on past performance) already included any considerations necessary for the firm's intellectual capital.

Regardless of why one might be interested in intellectual capital and its effect on stock price, let us begin the discussion with a brief review. Companies that make their profits by converting knowledge into value are called knowledge companies. Those companies whose profits come predominantly from commercializing innovations are at the core of the knowledge company definition. Microsoft, 3M, and IBM are examples of firms whose knowledge or intellectual capital is the firm's major asset. A knowledge company, whose profits come primarily from the commercialization of its ideas and innovations, possesses only two fundamental sources of value: its innovations and the complementary business assets of the firm that are applied to their commercialization. Further, there are only six ways that firms can convert innovations into profits: direct sale, out-licensing, joint venture to obtain and use needed complementary business assets, strategic alliance to obtain and exploit markets, integration, and donation (tax write-off).

For sophisticated knowledge companies, the route to maximizing profit extraction for any innovation is to maximize the number of combinations of unique complementary business assets and conversion mechanisms (see Exhibit 7.1).

The conversion mechanisms listed in Exhibit 7.1 are an all-inclusive set. Often the list is criticized as being too focused on companies whose intellectual capital is based in patents or other forms of intellectual property. While the list is more appropriate for IP than for uncodified knowledge, it applies as well to law firms and consulting firms as it does to technology companies.

All knowledge companies are comprised of the three major elements depicted in Exhibit 7.2. These companies are thought of as having intellectual capital and two forms of structural cap-

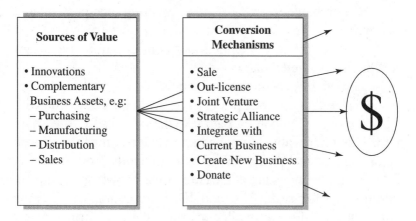

Exhibit 7.1 Sources of Value and Conversion Mechanisms in the Knowledge Company

Source: Patrick H. Sullivan, *Profiting from Intellectual Capital: Extracting Value from Innovation.* Copyright © 1998 by John Wiley & Sons, Inc. Reprinted by permission of John Wiley & Sons, Inc.

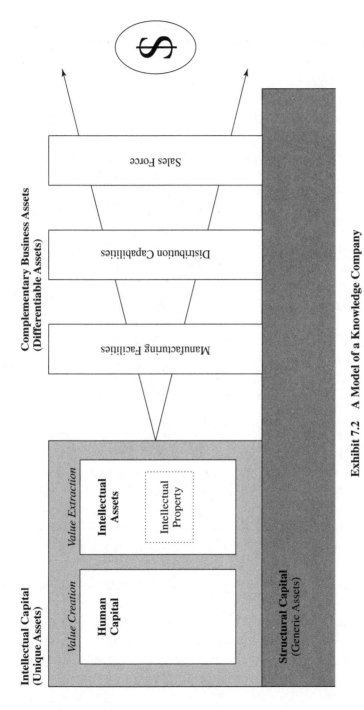

Exhibit 7.2   A Model of a Knowledge Company

Source: Patrick H. Sullivan, *Profiting from Intellectual Capital: Extracting Value from Innovation.*
Copyright © 1998 by John Wiley & Sons, Inc. Reprinted by permission of John Wiley & Sons, Inc.

ital. The first form is the generic structural capital that includes tangible assets that are widely undifferentiated and may be found generally in the marketplace. The second form of structural capital is the firm's complementary business assets (CBAs) which may be typically found in companies within the same industry. The particular form and capability of a firm's CBAs differentiate it from its sister companies in the industry.

The reason for re-introducing this model of a knowledge company into this chapter is that the three components of a knowledge company: IC, generic structural capital, and complementary business assets represent the three sources from which all companies create the value that subsequently is reflected in their income streams. As we shall see, these income streams have a major influence on stock price. (Note: knowledge companies, by definition, create their value either through their intellectual capital or their complementary business assets, or both.)

AN INTELLECTUAL CAPITAL APPROACH
TO VALUATION

The portion of the world's financial community that focuses on stock markets, as well as financial analysts and conceptual academics, has yet to develop models that describe the relationship between stock price (market capitalization divided by the number of shares of stock outstanding) and IC. At present the world's stock markets seem to believe that the value of a knowledge company is largely a function of the market's perceptions and beliefs about two significant things: the amount of intellectual capital the firm possesses and the firm's ability to leverage that intellectual capital in its marketplace. This leveraging factor represents the firm's ability to select the most commercializable innovations, to match them with the firm's business and marketing strategies, to determine how to match them with the firm's complementary business assets, which mechanisms to use to convert the innovations to cash, and then to make it all happen.

An intellectual capital (IC) approach to valuation differs significantly from the traditional accounting approaches. In the world of accounting, there are tangible assets and transaction-based prices. In the world of intellectual capital there are two sources of value: innovations (IC) and complementary business assets, and usually no transactions through which to value the assets directly. The differences between these two approaches are significant, but when valuing a knowledge company the IC approach offers a more accurate valuation than the business-asset approach.

The intellectual capital approach to valuation, because it recognizes that IC is one of the major sources of value for knowledge companies, tends to fully value the firm's intellectual capital. For companies wishing to convey information that fully informs about their value, the intellectual capital approach is much more informed than the more traditional accounting approach to valuation.

Generic Valuation Relationship

For companies whose value is largely due to their intangibles (the ideas and innovations of the employees), a tangible asset-based valuation may seriously understate the true value of the company. Let's look at two ways in which knowledge companies are valued in order to illustrate this point.

Acme Widget, a knowledge company, is publicly traded. The stock market, through Acme Widget's stock price, determines the current market value of the company. This value, sometimes called the market capitalization, reflects the market's view of two things. First, it reflects the market's understanding of the value of the firm's fixed assets, those found on the company's balance sheet. Second, it reflects the market's intuition or perception of both the amounts of Acme Widget's intellectual capital as well as its ability to leverage that IC in its marketplace. In contrast to the way in which the market views Acme Widget, let us look at the same elements of value from an IC perspective. First, the tangible assets of the firm are virtually the same as what the IC framework calls the firm's structural capital. Second, the market's perception of the firm's intellectual capital, when expressed in IC terms, means the expectation of future income from both the firm's innovations and the profits it will make by processing those innovations through the firm's complementary business assets.

For those who like to see relationships formalized in the form of an equation, the market value of a going concern (i.e., the stock price) may be expressed as:

$$Vm = VTA + DCF$$

where

$$Vm = \text{stock market value}$$

$$VTA = \text{the value of the firm's tangible assets}$$

$$DCF = \text{the value of the discounted future cash flows}$$
$$\text{the firm is expected to generate.}$$

This equation simply means that the value of a company is viewed as the sum of the value of its tangible assets (defined and valued on the company's balance sheet) and the net present value of the company's expected future cash flows (typically expressed as the firm's discounted cash flow or DCF).

We can also express the same relationship in intellectual capital terms in the following way:

$$Vm = Vsc + Vdcf_{ic}$$

where

$$Vm = \text{stock market value}$$

$$sc = \text{structural capital}$$

dcf_{ic} = discounted cash flows arising from the innovations of the company's IC

We must be careful to point out that it is *not* true that a company's value is equal to the sum of the value of the tangible assets and the intellectual capital. It *is* true that a knowledge firm's value is the sum of the value of its tangible assets and the discounted value of the cash flow that is generated largely by the firm's IC. In the case of intellectual capital companies, the IC creates the innovations that are used to generate cash flow. *Intellectual capital is the creator of cash flow!*

Knowledge Company Valuation Relationship

In Chapter 4 we saw the relationship between innovations and the cash flow they generate. This value chain discussion showed it is possible to identify the activities involved in converting an innovation into cash. The income stream generated by the firm's innovations is one of a knowledge firm's major sources of cash-based value. For companies like 3M, known for their ability to continually generate new innovations, one would expect most of their value to derive from their innovation-based income stream. In addition to the innovations of the firm's intellectual capital, another source of value for knowledge companies is the firm's complementary business assets. These assets, considered by economists to be the differentiable portion of the firm's structural capital, are a second source of profits for knowledge companies. Knowledge firms generating income from their complementary business assets, typically firms with large amounts of physical plant, can usually demonstrate that the cash flow produced by their complementary business assets comes about because of the unique relationship between these assets and the innovations of the firm's intellectual capital. Nevertheless, for firms such as these, it is the income stream from the CBAs that provides the cash-stream that affects the firm's stock price.

The third component of a knowledge firm is its generic structural capital. Although, in theory, these assets are not considered to be a source of value for knowledge companies, in practice they could be significant. Consider the case of GE Capital. This financial arm of General Electric has been the source of significant amounts of profit for the company in addition to profits generated by its intellectual capital and its complementary business assets.

In any formula used to forecast the earnings of a firm, three terms must be included: a term for the earnings stream associated with the income generated by the firm's innovations or intellectual capital, a term to account for the earnings generated by the firm's complementary business assets, and finally a term to account for any earnings associated with the firm's generic structural capital. Such an equation for total earnings might look like the following:

$$V_m = V_{TA} + \text{NPV of earnings from the firm's intellectual capital}$$
$$+ \text{NPV of earnings from the firm's complementary business assets}$$
$$+ \text{NPV of earnings from the firm's generic structural capital}$$

A more traditional version of the above relationships between value and its sources would look more like:

$$V_m = V_{TA} + \text{NPV} \begin{pmatrix} \text{Earnings IC}_A \\ + \\ \text{Earnings IC}_B \\ + \\ \vdots \\ \text{Earnings IC}_N \end{pmatrix} + \text{NPV} \begin{pmatrix} \text{Earnings CBA}_i \\ + \\ \text{Earnings CBA}_j \\ + \\ \vdots \\ \text{Earnings IC}_P \end{pmatrix} + \text{NPV} \begin{pmatrix} \text{Earnings GSC}_q \\ + \\ \text{Earnings GSC}_r \\ + \\ \vdots \\ \text{Earnings GSC}_z \end{pmatrix}$$

where

V_m = Market value (market capitalization) of the firm

V_{TA} = The value of the firm's tangible assets

IC = Innovations of the firm's intellectual capital (where A–Z are specific groupings of IC)

CBA = Complementary business assets (where A–Z are the specific CBAs associated with each grouping of IC)

GSC = Generic structural capital

Several things should be said about the above equation. First, concerning the value of the firm's tangible assets, purists might argue that because some of these assets are involved with the generation of earnings, counting them here may be a doubling of their value. While this is surely true, as a practical matter most knowledge firms find that the value of their tangible assets is quite small in proportion with their tangible assets. For firms such as this, simply including all of the tangible assets in the equation for value may be a time-saving step that introduces no significant change to its value. Firms whose value includes a substantial portion from tangible assets should spend the time to separate those that are involved with creating the firm's income streams from those that are not.

Second, firms wishing to positively affect stock price and whose value derives largely from their IC-generated income should emphasize to investors and financial analysts all of the aspects of their IC that are used to create the firm's income streams. Equally, for firms whose source of value lies with their complementary business assets, the approach to investors and analysts should emphasize the income streams emanating from their business assets. Completing the set, firms whose sources of value derive from combinations of intellectual capital and complementary business assets should stress the income streams that come from these combinations, with investors or financial analysts.

Third, when a firm finds that its major source of value comes from the income streams generated from its generic structural capital, it should recognize that the stock market is unlikely to see them as a knowledge company. Indeed, the market will see the company for what it is, a going concern whose profits arise from some application of its generic assets.

SUMMARY

The ability to leverage ideas into cash flow varies from one company to the next. Some companies do this very well, others not well. But if one believes that intellectual capital may be the driver of a firm's cash flow, then it is possible to forecast the income streams and earnings that result from each of the firm's three kinds of assets: intellectual capital, complementary business assets, and generic structural capital. By identifying the kinds of value that a firm wishes to obtain from its intellectual capital, it is possible to know how the firm might manage its IC to produce the desired results (value chains are helpful to determine what activities are required to convert innovations into desired kinds of value). Once a set of value chains has been created, it becomes possible to forecast the income associated with each.

As we have discussed in this chapter, if stock price is a function of the value of a firm's tangible assets plus the net present value of its income streams, it becomes possible to define and describe the relationships that significantly affect the firm's income streams, its earnings, and thereby its stock price.

Part III

Managing
Intellectual Capital

8

Extracting Value
from Intellectual Property

For technology companies, a well-constructed system for managing intellectual properties is fundamental to extracting full value from the properties *and* to creating IA and IC management systems to extract value successfully from all three tiers of the firm's intellectual capital. Several companies (IBM, Dow Chemical, and Texas Instruments) are noted for their ability to manage their intellectual properties in order to extract significant amounts of cash value from them. In this area, technology companies have an advantage over service firms or firms that do not hold a portfolio of intellectual properties. Technology firms can develop the decision processes, databases, and work processes required to successfully extract value from their intellectual properties. In so doing, these firms create the culture, structure, and decision-making capability for systematically extracting value from their intangibles. With the building block of an IP management capability in place, it is easy for firms to expand it to encompass their intellectual assets and finally their human capital. Lacking the foundation of an IP management system, firms typically do not extract the degree of value from all of their intellectual capital they otherwise would be capable of.

Because of the increased value of intellectual property in general and patents in particular, knowledge companies must ask themselves whether they are using these valuable assets to their best advantage. How are these assets being managed? How are they being exploited to improve the firm's position in the marketplace? How are they being used to improve the firm's position in relation to that of its competitors?

This chapter discusses the methods and systems that companies have effectively used to link their intellectual property with their business strategy as well as methods for extracting the most value from intellectual properties themselves. It is intended to be a primer for patent attorneys, general counsels, and senior executives about how to change the way in which the firm views the commercialization and positioning opportunities available through intellectual property. This chapter is about intellectual property management and the creation of a set of core management capabilities upon which the other tiers of intellectual capital management may be based.

HISTORICAL PERSPECTIVE

Intellectual assets that receive legal protection are called *intellectual property*. Intellectual property law, the body of law dealing with the protection of intellectual assets, recognizes five forms of legal protection in the United States: patents, copyrights, trademarks, trade secrets, and semiconductor masks. For each form of protection, the nature and amount of protection available as well as the degree to which that protection applies to an innovation may vary.

For firms holding patents, the most usual form of protection that companies actively manage, some significant changes have taken place since the late 1980s. Before that time, the judicial environment was decidedly anti-patent. The U.S. Supreme Court was generally anti-monopoly and anti-patent during the so-called Black/Douglas era (1946–1965). The chances of a patent's being held valid, infringed, and enforceable in litigation were only about one in three. Moreover, the U.S. Department of Justice (DOJ) subscribed to the view that patents were bad monopolies that stifled competition in the marketplace by preventing companies from copying each other's products. Companies using their patent and technology prowess aggressively sometimes found themselves the subject of a governmentally enforced consent decree requiring low or zero patent royalty payments to competitors.

This state of affairs made an about-face in the early 1980s. The report of the President's Commission on Industrial Competitiveness identified intellectual property as one of four critical areas for achieving and maintaining competitiveness in American industry. A new court of appeals for the Federal Circuit was created to unify legal precedent in patent cases, which was previously fragmented among the eleven circuit courts of appeal. Antitrust restrictions were relaxed; the National Cooperative Research Act (1984) became law and permitted competitors to do joint research more freely.

Subsequent to 1982 and the creation of the new court of appeals, the number of significant domestic and international intellectual property cases heard, as well as the dollar amounts of settlements, make it clear that intellectual property has become an asset of significant value. The market value of patents has increased; their value in business negotiations has gone up; and their significance as a major source of value for knowledge firms has increased.

EXTRACTING VALUE
FROM INTELLECTUAL PROPERTIES

The effective management of and extraction of value from intellectual property are activities associated with the third dimension of the IC framework: IC activities. To effectively manage and extract value from its portfolio the firm needs to understand that there are several *dimensions* to a portfolio of IP. There is a time or *current vs. future* dimension associated with the tiers of intellectual capital. Intellectual properties may be thought of as the source of *current* value for the firm. Much of what is currently in the portfolio is the basis for protecting current products in the marketplace, or current joint ventures and strategic alliances. Intellectual properties represent current value where the value-extraction activities are rife with tactical considerations. Intellectual assets, the next tier of intellectual capital, have less current definition, and often more promise for the future. Extracting value from these assets usually involves thinking into the future, discussing positioning and strategies for value extraction rather than near-term tactics. For this reason, intellectual assets are usually considered to be assets that bridge the transition from the present to the future (also from the tactical to the strategic) value extraction. The intellectual capital tier, to complete the thought, operates almost entirely at the strategic level of decision-making and future value extraction, but uses the same fundamental decision processes as those found in the most fundamental and well-constructed systems for extracting value from intellectual property.

There are at least two widely held and different philosophical views of the function of IP management, and these philosophies fundamentally shape the context within which portfolio use is viewed. One view is that the portfolio's highest and best use is to protect the firm's innovations from competitive attack (the portfolio-as-protection view). Other uses of the portfolio, proponents argue, might direct energies away from the firm's main business—commercializing innovation. The contrasting view (the portfolio-as-business-asset view) is that the portfolio is a great source of corporate value for firms willing to exploit it. Companies that hold this latter view believe that the portfolio has the potential to significantly enhance the value of the firm.

For many firms, extracting new or extra value from their intellectual properties means a shift in focus away from a *portfolio-as-protection-only* view to a *portfolio-as-corporate-business-asset* view. This shift in perspective opens up more alternative ways to use the portfolio for the firm's benefit and thereby allows firms to create more value-extraction opportunities. For example, a manufacturing firm making the shift in perspective might find it has opened up new opportunities for out-licensing it never considered before; it might find new strategic alliance opportunities or joint venture opportunities. But, to *maximize* value extraction from the portfolio, firms must go a step further. Value maximization involves the creation of a full range of value extraction mechanisms and their *simultaneous use* with individual technologies. Such a manufacturing company might find itself simultaneously manufacturing and distributing a technology application in the North American market, licensing it to manufacturers in the South American market, doing a joint venture with Asian manufacturers or distributors, and entering a strategic alliance with one or more European companies, *all involving the same technology innovation, and all at the same time!*

The Portfolio as Protection

Companies with this (largely defensive) view oppose the idea that the IP portfolio should be used for any strategic purpose other than protecting the firm's innovations. They believe that the portfolio's use should be restricted to achieving the four primary objectives for patenting. Their overarching goal is to exclude others from using their patented innovations. These companies are often decentralized and structured around strategic business units (SBUs). Their profits are created in the near term through the sales of the products and services of the SBUs. For the most part, the business units in these firms own the innovations: they decide what is to be patented and how those patents will be used. For these companies, patenting is primarily a legal and a local business issue and is often managed or coordinated by the SBUs and the firm's office of general counsel.

The Portfolio as a Corporate Asset

Companies that take a more aggressive view use their portfolios to create superior value. These companies believe that extracting value from their protected innovations is not limited to bringing a better mousetrap to the market. For example, a company may decide to license its mousetrap technology to others for manufacturing and distribution because it does not have the required capabilities itself. Similarly, it may enter into a joint venture with another company, set up a strategic alliance with a partner that can give it access to markets it might otherwise be unable to reach, or simply sell a technology in which it no longer has a strategic interest. Such companies take a broad view of their patent portfolios. They seek to extract value from the portfolio by treating it as a collective corporate asset rather than as a collection of individual patents.

It requires more than a shift in perspective for firms to *maximize* their value extraction. It requires a shift in context. It requires the firm to realize that it is no longer in the technology-application manufacturing business. It is in the business of commercializing technology. Companies able to shift their context or, in other words, their self-view, are companies with the strategic perspective necessary to fully extract value from all of their intellectual assets. This chapter is written for companies capable of shifting their context about commercializing their intellectual properties. It discusses methods and systems for effectively linking intellectual property with business strategy as well as methods for extracting the most value from the intellectual properties themselves.

Extracting value from intellectual property is accomplished most effectively when the value extraction activities meet two criteria. First, they must be aimed at improving the firm's competitive position as defined in the corporate business strategy.

Second, they must become part of a systematized set of decision processes supported with information-producing activities and databases that collectively allow the firm to manage its IP assets.

Knowledge firms usually think of value extraction in terms of converting an innovation into cash or profits. Indeed, any activity that increases income or reduces expenses (or both) while requiring few resources to do so may be considered an attractive value-extraction alternative. Extracting value from intellectual properties, because of its strong current time-frame and tactical focus, is usually thought of as a near- to mid-term profitability opportunity. But what are some of these profit-generating activities?

Short-Term Value Extraction

Corporations that want to extract value from or improve the profitability of their portfolios immediately have at least two courses of action available to them: (1) reduce portfolio expense by reducing the amount of patent maintenance taxes, and (2) increase portfolio income by improving the royalty income stream from out-licenses.

Reducing Portfolio Expense

Much of the expense of maintaining a patent portfolio comes in the form of patent maintenance fees or taxes. Starting in 1993, the Dow Chemical Company, in a sustained drive to lower these costs, reduced its annual costs for obtaining and maintaining patents by $1.5 million. It accomplished this by aligning the patents in its portfolio with the firm's business strategies. As a result, Dow was able to eliminate patents and reduce the size of its portfolio from 12,000 patents in 1993 to 8,500 in 1999. Dow estimates that this process resulted in a $40 million tax maintenance savings over a lifetime/average of 10 years for the portfolio. For most firms, it is not unusual to find that approximately 5 percent of the patents in the portfolio are no longer useful and could be eliminated. Thus, just by reviewing their portfolios, many firms could realize immediate savings of about 5 percent per year in maintenance fees.

Increasing Portfolio Income

In general, companies that have out-licensed their technologies receive far less in royalty payments than they expected based on the terms contained in the firm's licensing agreements. This should not be surprising. Licensees under cash management pressure create reasons why they need not make their royalty payments immediately. For example, some licensees say they are holding the royalty payments in an accrual account until the licensor asks for it; others say that they are having cash flow problems and decided to defer payment (without notifying the licensor). Still others make payments, but of a lesser amount than called for. In the latter case the mere announcement of a licensor's intent to audit royalty payments often produces an unsolicited check for back payment of royalties owed. Firms that audit their royalty income usually find that the amount of income received as a result of the audit far outweighs its cost.

Mid-Term Value Extraction

Whereas the short term is viewed as the forthcoming year, the mid-term is defined here as meaning a two- to four-year period. During this mid-term period, value extraction activities focus on: increasing portfolio quality; increasing use of the portfolio in business negotiations; and expanding licensing, joint venturing, and strategic alliance activities.

One way to increase portfolio quality is to develop a screen for filtering out patents that do not bring value to the company's portfolio. Each patent in the portfolio should be included for clear reasons that relate to specific elements of the firm's business tactics or strategy.

As the portfolio improves in quality it will probably contain fewer total patents but more usable ones. With increasing quality, the portfolio brings more strength to the company's bargaining position in cross-licensing discussions, in discussions with potential litigants, and in a whole range of negotiating situations.

With an enhanced portfolio there are new opportunities for out-licensing, joint venturing, and the creative and market exploration of strategic alliances.

A HIERARCHY OF IP ACTIVITY

Julie L. Davis, co-leader of Arthur Andersen's Intellectual Asset Management practice, developed a simple graphic that helps companies compare themselves against a "yardstick" related to the management of their intellectual assets. The graphic, which Arthur Andersen calls IP Value Hierarchy (see Exhibit 8.1), describes a series of levels of activity and use for the firms' intellectual property.[1]

Defensive Level

This is the most fundamental of IP functions. It characterizes the view held by most large corporations up to the early 1980s.

Exhibit 8.1   The Arthur Andersen IP Value Hierarchy

Companies at this level are compliance-oriented and reactive in nature. Their primary purpose for IP is to create a shield to protect the company from litigation. These companies hope that by creating a "pile of patents" bigger than their competitors, they can protect themselves from litigation because they will be able to negotiate cross-licenses rather than go to court.

Cost Control Level

Companies at this second level are focused on how to reduce the costs of filing and maintaining their patent portfolios. Well-executed strategies at this level can save the company millions of dollars annually. Such strategies typically include periodic and conscientious pruning of the patent portfolio to save unnecessary maintenance fees, more deliberate decision-making regarding the countries in which to file, and consolidation of the foreign patent agent costs.

Profit Center Level

The focus of company IP activities at the third level shifts from cost control to revenue maximization. This level of IP activity is characterized by more proactive strategies. Individual business units relinquish control over their IP assets to a consolidated, usually central, IP function. Though individual business units may continue to own the IP, the centralized IP function is held accountable for the performance of IP licensing as a revenue-generating activity, becomes strategic for companies at this level. Hence, portfolio mining and patent enforcement become of interest to companies at this level.

Integration Level

At the fourth level of activity, IP ceases to focus exclusively on self-centered activities and reaches outwardly beyond its own department to serve a greater purpose within the firm. In essence, firms at this level of IP sophistication have integrated their IP activities with those of other functions and embedded them in the day-to-day operations, procedures, and strategies of the company. As a result, the IP function contributes to decisions made by executives with responsibilities in research and development (R&D), human resources, treasury, mergers and acquisitions, etc.

Visionary Level

Few companies reach the fifth level of IP activity. Here, IP activities are strategically focused, looking outside the company and into the future. The IP function within companies at this level of sophistication takes on the challenge of identifying future trends in customer preferences as well as future trends in the industry. They actively seek to position the corporation as a leader in its field, by acquiring or developing the IP necessary to protect the company's margins and market share in the future.

THE ROLES OF INTELLECTUAL PROPERTY IN CORPORATE BUSINESS STRATEGY

As stated above, companies create intellectual property portfolios for one major competitive purpose: near-term competitive advantage. For technology-based companies this translates into three objectives: protection for innovations, design freedom, and litigation avoidance. For companies capable of shifting to a portfolio-as-corporate-asset view (the new and more expansive view of the firm's portfolio), the list of objectives is expanded to include the creation of a basis for establishing alliances and joint ventures. Technology-based businesses create portfolios of technology that are fundamentally a collection of innovative ideas for whose use the company wishes to be granted a legal monopoly. In most cases the individual patents, trademarks, and other protected assets are intended to generate near-term income by providing limited protection to a mark, a product, or process innovation to allow its commercialization without fear of imitation. As companies grow and produce improved and new innovations, they often build a significant portfolio of patents and other intellectual properties.

IP Strategy and Company Strategy

Whether a company's IP strategy is or should be offensive or defensive in nature depends in large measure on the company's business strategy and the role intellectual property is expected to play in that strategy. Returning to fundamentals, the company has a vision of what it wishes to become in the future. This vision establishes a long-term goal in order to focus employee day-to-day activity. For knowledge companies, the firm's strategy, the set of decisions about the strategic issues affecting progress toward the vision, includes the role the firm's intellectual capital is expected to contribute.

The roles of intellectual capital are typically specified for both value-creation and value-extraction (see Exhibit 8.2). This chapter focuses on the value-extraction activities, in particular those relating to the firm's intellectual property and its management.

For firms that expect intellectual property to play a significant role in the corporate strategy or for firms with a significant number of intellectual properties, an IP strategy can guide employee decision-making on issues and outcomes that will move the firm toward its strategic vision. IP strategies are particularly helpful when they outline the strategic objectives of the firm and its related IP activity as well as the expected use to which the firm's IP is to be put.

Breadth of IP Strategy

Strategic objectives and use may vary considerably depending upon the business strategy of the firm.

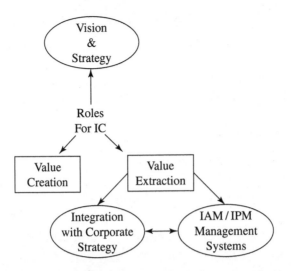

Exhibit 8.2   Relationships among Vision, Strategy, and Intellectual Capital

Source: Patrick H. Sullivan, *Profiting from Intellectual Capital: Extracting Value from Innovation*. Copyright © 1998 by John Wiley & Sons, Inc. Reprinted by permission of John Wiley & Sons, Inc.

A company with a *broadly focused business strategy* focuses on technologies that can be developed and patented in anticipation of some future use. The portfolio is created with an expectation that it can contribute to the creation of some future market demand. The corollary of this is that often a technology is patented in order to stake out an early claim to future design freedom. Companies with a broadly focused business strategy tend to be strategically opportunistic.

A company with a *narrowly focused business strategy* uses targeted R&D to develop technologies that will meet a known or narrowly defined current (or potential) market demand. The time horizon for commercialization typically is short. Companies in this group tend to cull their portfolios routinely to ensure that the portfolio's contents continue to be tightly arranged around the focused business strategy.

In most firms the patent portfolio is an outgrowth of the firm's business strategy and merits the attention from senior managers that would be expected for a valued corporate asset. In firms such as these there is usually a well-articulated set of definitions of the firm's strategic objectives for its intellectual properties as well as the use to which those properties are expected to be put.

Strategic Objectives and Intent

All companies with patent portfolios create them with an expectation of how they will be used in the near term and in future technology-based opportunities:

1. *Protection from competition.* The holder of a patent is granted a fundamental monopoly right that prohibits others from commercializing the patented technology without express permission from the patent holder.

2. *Complementary protection.* Some patents are developed with no view toward direct commercialization. They provide complementary protection for a similar innovation but are created using different materials or processes. Complementary groups of patents formed around a key patent afford it a higher degree of protection and guard against thicket formation by competitors.

3. *Design freedom and litigation avoidance.* A portfolio often contains patents on future technologies, created in order to ensure that the firm has a prior claim to a specific area of technology. It signals that the firm is seriously in business in this area and can be expected to defend its intellectual property position forcefully. These prior claims are made to ensure the ability to commercialize new technologies over an extended period of time without threat of infringement.

4. *Basis for alliances.* An alliance is any business relationship formed with another party to meet a critical business need, including market access, product line expansion, technol-

ogy transfer, and manufacturing competency. As customer demands become more complex, so do the technologies and services required to create solutions that will sell in the marketplace. Since no single company is likely to have expertise in the ever-widening span of technology, putting together a winning market solution often requires putting together a partnership or an alliance.

A large and strong portfolio and the means to continue generating large numbers of quality innovations is a measure of the technological and commercial strength of a technology-based firm. This can be a major advantage when seeking alliance partners who themselves are looking for a company with strengths to complement their own.

Strategic Use

While strategic intent focuses on what the firm wants to happen in the future, strategic use focuses on portfolio activity in the present. Strategic use may be thought of in terms of business opportunities, either those currently being pursued or those to be pursued in the near future. Portfolios are structured mainly for offensive and defensive strategic uses, but often are put to other uses such as establishing strong negotiating positions and enhancing the technological stature of the firm.

1. *Offensive use of the portfolio.* Offensive use includes both direct commercialization and tactical blocking. Direct commercialization can be achieved by clustering groups of patents together in estates around planned or future products, around the core competencies of the firm, or both. These estates are aimed at producing a proprietary position in specific product areas. Offensive estates can also be clusters of improvements formed in a picket fence or thicket around the foundation patents of a competitor or a potential licensor. Offensive use usually involves

excluding competitors from using the technology or business application for the life of the patent. Through careful use of licensing to excluded competitors, a firm may use the portfolio offensively to gain partial access to markets not otherwise within its reach. Similarly, a firm might develop alliances to gain access to needed technologies or markets.

2. *Defensive use of the portfolio.* Defensive uses tend to require a broad array of patents covering future uses of technology, processes, and materials that broadly cover as-yet-undefined products. In addition to ensuring exclusive use of a technology, defensive use of the portfolio usually means ensuring design freedom for the future. Successful defensive use also avoids litigation resulting from cross-licensing and other related strategic moves.

3. *Negotiation.* For the most part, firms interested in using the portfolio in negotiations have developed it in one of two ways. A portfolio may contain a set of patents focused around a specific technology or business area. Firms negotiating a cross-licensing agreement or a business arrangement can be aided by the mere existence of a highly focused portfolio with strengths in the area of interest of both firms in the negotiation. Alternatively, the creation of a large brood portfolio including both existing and potential technologies can itself be intimidating to a negotiating firm.

4. *Enhancing the technological image of the firm.* A large and strong portfolio and the means and will to continue generating large numbers of quality patents is a measure and indication of the technological and commercial stature of the firm. This is a factor in seeking joint venture partners and in the silent effect a strong portfolio (and the ability to continuously regenerate it) has on potentially infringing competitors.

The development of an IP strategy for the firm, in addition to focusing its scope on activities associated with the firm's intellectual property, must also be focused on supporting the long-term business strategy, which itself is supporting the achievement of the strategic vision. The logic behind the development of a firm's IP strategy includes *a priori* review of the firm's vision and corporate strategy and the identification of the roles intellectual capital and its subset, intellectual property, may play. The roles available for intellectual property may then be codified into a set of activities and practices which themselves are the foundation of the firm's IP strategy.

THE INTELLECTUAL PROPERTY MANAGEMENT SYSTEM

Strategy implementation inevitably involves many parts of the organization. In a knowledge firm, many daily activities are concerned with maintaining the portfolio. Some of these involve improving the flow of potential patents into the patenting decision process; others relate to the cost management of the portfolio; the processes of valuing patents; and determining the optimum set of conversion mechanisms for extracting value from a patent the firm has decided to commercialize. With this bustle of activity, mass confusion is a distinct possibility unless the firm creates a systematic way of conducting each of these activities in its own time frame and coordinated with the others. Such a capability is often thought of as a system. Systems are describable, their flows and processes are explicit, their relationships to one another are visible, and the requirements for each system are relatable to the company's business strategy.

The management of a complex series of activities such as those described for managing the firm's intellectual property, requires a system and a systematic approach. Anything less leads to chaos, misunderstanding, and wasted effort.

COMPONENTS OF AN INTELLECTUAL PROPERTY MANAGEMENT (IPM) SYSTEM

Managing intellectual property involves a series of activities and functions, each necessary to provide the basic information on which business decisions may be made, decisions about specific pieces of intellectual property that activate the link between individual patents in the portfolio and the company's business strategy.

How should the firm's intellectual property manager conceive and direct this series of activities and functions? The answer lies in understanding not only what the functions of IP management are but also what capabilities a firm must develop in order to make the functions happen. A complete generic IP management system (as shown in Exhibit 8.3) has five areas of responsibility.

Generation of Candidate Intellectual Properties

This includes all activities associated with identifying potential innovations, analysis, categorization, and the decision to patent. The elements of the generation portion of an IPM system include:

1. *Overseeing the innovation process.* IPM includes monitoring the firm's innovation management activity: stages of innovation, decision processes, status of development for key innovations. Firms with strong IPM have usually institutionalized the innovation process, defining and describing the serial stages of research, innovation, development, and product creation. The management of innovation for these firms includes evaluating the progress of innovations toward commercialization, re-evaluating the strategic importance of each innovation in conjunction with the business plan, determining the amount of investment required for commercialization, and deciding whether to continue or cancel the innovation's development process.

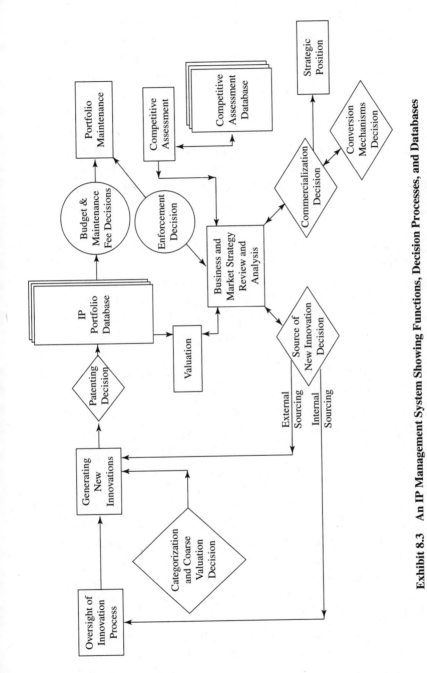

Exhibit 8.3   An IP Management System Showing Functions, Decision Processes, and Databases

Source: Patrick H. Sullivan, *Profiting from Intellectual Capital: Extracting Value from Innovation.*
Copyright © 1998 by John Wiley & Sons, Inc. Reprinted by permission of John Wiley & Sons, Inc.

2. *Generating new patents.* Because the decision to patent a technology has so many implications for the firm, it is one of the fundamental decisions a technology-based knowledge company can make. It determines the basis from which product and process applications are developed and subsequently sold. This decision more than any other determines the future course of the company. It can affect the quality (utility) of the patent portfolio; the future cost of maintaining the portfolio; the business strategy in those cases where a business is based on one or more technologies; and the company's legal or protection strategy. For all of these reasons, successful companies carefully consider the selection of innovations to become part of their patent portfolio.

The generation of patentable innovations must be preceded by identifying the technology areas in which new or more patents are desired; providing the incentives necessary for generating an amount of patent requests sufficient to meet the company's needs; and creating screening criteria and decision processes for deciding which of the patent requests to pursue and which to drop.

Each potentially patentable innovation should be analyzed twice, first from a technical perspective and then from a business perspective. The technical analysis is conducted to determine the technical merits from the firm's perspective: Is the technology consistent with the firm's technical strengths? Does it add to the firm's technical position? Is it a technology the firm will wish to pursue in the future? Would staking out a technological interest in a new area be beneficial to the firm in the future?

Business-oriented analysis of a potential patent might include concerns about the market acceptance of applications developed from the technology. Would the products or processes that evolve from applications of the technology be in the firm's current or planned areas of business? Would products or processes resulting from the technology require new investment? If so, how much? What level of income would these products generate? When could that income stream begin?

There are other business-oriented questions that may be asked. What are the intended business uses for the patent (e.g., direct commercialization, protecting some other business asset, use as an anti-competitive weapon)? What would be the ability of the patent to exclude others (e.g., excellent, nominal, poor)? How easy would it be to detect infringement of the patent (that is, would infringement be visibly detectable, or would the technology be used inside another apparatus, making infringement neither visible nor easy to detect)?

3. *Patent categorization decision process.* Many of the selection criteria may also be used to qualitatively value the patent once it is issued and placed in the company's patent portfolio. The *value grid*, described later in this chapter, is a useful method for categorizing patents.

Portfolio Management

Most companies maintain patents in their portfolio throughout the life of the patent and pay the patent maintenance fees required to maintain the patent in force. Successful patent managers, however, routinely review their budgets for maintenance fee payments and cull their portfolios of properties that once offered value to the firm but no longer do so. The portfolio is routinely screened for patents no longer of value to the firm and payment of maintenance fees on these is discontinued. Companies that actively manage and maintain their portfolios report dramatic reduction in portfolio maintenance fees. Two types of decisions to be made regarding patent management are as follows:

1. *Budget and maintenance fee decisions.* The costs associated with maintaining patents can be high. Many compa-

nies, because of the design of their accounting system, do not even know the actual costs. Nevertheless, the cost of obtaining and maintaining patents is considerable and should represent a firm's conscious decision to invest in the creation and generation of technology products that will create future income.

In order to make rational decisions about the costs, companies should budget funds for this purpose and assign a portfolio manager to ensure that this and other portfolio goals are met. The portfolio manager may present management with tradeoffs related to managing the portfolio. For example, it may make sense to discontinue the maintenance on some less-useful patents in the portfolio in order to make funds available for new technologies with more potential for contributing to the firm's capabilities in the marketplace.

2. *Patent enforcement decisions.* When infringement of a company's patented technology has been detected, the firm must decide how to enforce its rights. The relevant considerations include the company's context, its competitive position, the effect enforcement could have on customers' perceptions of the firm, the strength of an enforcement action, the nature and kind of resolution to be sought through an enforcement action, the probability of success, and more. Enforcement decisions are often significant enough to be made at the firm's strategic level.

IP Valuation

Knowledge firms are routinely faced with a need to value their technologies, patented or not, and inevitably a portfolio manager is asked to value one or more patents in the portfolio. A significant new function that technology-based knowledge firms are adding to their management system capability is the ability to produce valuations of their technology.

Competitive Assessment

This function involves the development, assimilation, and promulgation of information on both business and technology competitors.

Strategic Decision-Making

The analysis of intellectual properties to determine whether and how to commercialize them for the benefit of the firm is the strategic decision-making function within IPM. Using the firm's business strategy as the guide, managers evaluate properties for their commercial use. A decision may be reached to either commercialize, or store the technology for future use until another technology becomes available that will make the initial technology more appropriate to commercialize. These two alternatives are explained in more depth as follows:

1. *Commercialization decisions.* In a sophisticated IPM company, the commercialization decision is largely anti-climactic. In such companies, innovations under development have been continuously tracked and evaluated. Increasingly detailed analyses have determined the market need, the degree of market acceptance, the complementary assets required for commercialization, access to those assets, and the most appropriate conversion mechanisms.

2. *Defining the need for more technology.* A firm uses the results of the business and marketing strategy analysis along with the competitive assessment information to determine whether its competitive position could be improved through the addition of a specific technology to its portfolio. If it determines that a patented technology is unsuitable for commercialization, it is usually for one of the following reasons:
   - The expected market for applications of the technology has not materialized or is not adequate to support further

149

investment. In this case the firm should seek other or related technological innovations which, when paired with the one under examination, could demonstrate acceptable levels of market acceptance.

- *The innovation cannot be adequately protected legally.* In this case the firm should seek to pair this technology with others that have greater ability to qualify for legal protection in order to proceed with commercialization.

In either case, the firm seeks other technologies to match with the technology under review. Outside the company there may be a licensable technology residing with a firm that can be merged with or acquired, or there may be people available for hire who have the requisite skills or knowledge to create the technology directly. Alternatively, the firm may have the ability to create the new technology itself. In either case, the sourcing decision is one that, like the enforcement decision, sometimes requires strategic decision-making.

ALTERNATIVE METHODS OF PROTECTION (EXTRA-LEGAL)

Legal protection is only one of several ways to give the firm a monopoly-like position and thereby capture value from the innovation. In extracting value, strategy and positioning are usually more important than protection. Patents are crucial in some industries, such as chemicals and more recently, electronics. In other industries, such as semiconductors, speed in getting the product to market is the most important factor in maximizing sales revenue. The difference by industry allows us to divide the world into two regimes, according to the strength of the legal protection available to the innovating firm. An industry with good intellectual property protection operates under one regime, and an industry or technological area with poor intellectual property protection (i.e., where imitation is easy) operates under another. This chapter so far has focused on firms in the first regime, where good intellectual property protection is available.

For firms without good intellectual property protection, other, non-legal methods for developing a near-monopoly position may exist, but they must have the required complementary business assets.

Specific complementary assets are unique to a product or technology and can be used strategically to isolate a technology from competitors and extract more value. For example, manufacturing facilities capable of handling rapid growth while maintaining high quality constitute an extremely valuable complementary asset. Thus, Compaq Computer was able to grow rapidly in the MS-DOS personal computer (PC) market in the 1980s at the expense of technological pioneer IBM, largely because IBM lacked the critical manufacturing assets to meet the PC demand it had created. Because Compaq quickly recognized and took advantage of complementary capability necessary for success in the PC market, it was rewarded with rapid market penetration.

Thus, where firms can limit their rivals' access to complementary assets, they can significantly slow down the rate of competition. Imitators desiring to enter the marketplace must not only replicate the technology of the product; they must also develop the complementary assets required to commercialize the technology. When AT&T tried to enter the PC business in 1984, it lacked the marketing assets (sales force and distribution systems) necessary to support PC products. The lack of these assets and the time AT&T spent trying to acquire them may explain why, four years and $2.5 billion later, AT&T still had not become a viable competitor to Compaq and IBM in the PC marketplace.

Because specific complementary assets are usually created in conjunction with the commercialization of one specific application of an innovation and are therefore unique, they are often themselves able to be protected. In effect, controlling the specific complementary assets is equivalent to controlling the underlying intellectual capital.

Thus, ownership of specific complementary business assets may often provide reasonable or adequate de facto protection when legal protection is not available. A corollary is that if the complementary asset is critical and unattainable, a firm that can find an unconventional way of eliminating it can also be advantaged. For example, when Canon was exploring the introduction of a new line of copiers in the U.S. market, it realized that it lacked an adequate distribution network to service them. In a creative use of technology, Canon redesigned the machines' toner cartridge, making its replacement the equivalent of a service call, and eliminated the need for a service network.

SUMMARY

Intellectual property management is a key set of concepts, methods, and processes designed for aligning the intellectual properties of the firm with its business strategies and objectives. It represents one of the fundamental approaches to maximizing the extraction of value from a firm's intellectual capital.

Companies engaged with technology have the advantage of two forms of intangible assets not available to non-technology companies. Technology-based companies can extract value from both intellectual assets and intellectual properties. Companies with intellectual properties may create a portfolio of IP assets to use defensively (portfolio-as-protection) or offensively (portfolio-as-corporate-asset).

A firm that wants to maximize the value extracted from its portfolio of intellectual properties must have several key elements in place. First, it must have a clearly defined and well-articulated vision as well as a strategy for achieving the vision. In addition, a knowledge of the firm's actual and desired values is desirable in order to ensure their consistency with the values and strategy. Second, it is important for the firm to develop a clear portfolio strategy, one that identifies the defensive and offensive elements of portfolio use. Third, the firm must clearly identify the role(s) intellectual property is to play in the strategy and then create a plan for moving IPM toward its strategic capability.

An intellectual property management system must contain the key elements described in this chapter and must also identify key decisions and define decision-making processes, including who is involved, what information is needed by the decision-makers, what work processes are necessary to provide this information, what databases are needed to store the information, and how each decision will be implemented.

NOTE

1. Davis, J., "Using Your IP to Increase Shareholder Value," *Patent Yearbook 1998*, Economy Publications PLC, London, 1998.

9

Extracting Value
from Intellectual Assets

Extracting value from intellectual assets, the company's codified knowledge, builds upon the system for extracting value from intellectual property. Intellectual asset management (IAM) is similar to intellectual property management (IPM) in that it uses the same conceptual basis that specifies innovation and complementary assets as the primary sources of value for the firm. It also uses the same conversion mechanisms for converting value into profits. But IAM differs from IPM in at least three significant ways. First, the unprotected commercializable assets, when added to the protected commercializable assets, constitute a set of interactive intellectual assets that is significantly more complex to coordinate and manage. Second, whereas IPM is focused on current extraction from assets currently or soon to be in the portfolio, IAM is concerned with less well defined assets that have the potential to generate income. Third, whereas extracting value from intellectual property is *tactically* focused, and extracting value from intellectual capital is *strategically* focused, extracting value from intellectual assets lies between the two, having both tactical and strategic implications.

This chapter discusses intellectual assets: what they are, the differences between commercializable and non-commercializable

IAs, the differences between IAs that are managed for direct commercialization and IAs that become part of the firm's structural capital and thereby indirectly support commercialization. The chapter also discusses how intellectual assets are valued, how they are managed, and how profits may be extracted from them.

INTELLECTUAL ASSETS

Knowledge

Successful knowledge companies create sustainable value through the creation of knowledge and know-how. Some of that knowledge and know-how becomes codified and forms intellectual assets; the remainder is tacit knowledge that remains within the human capital. It is to the advantage of knowledge firms to institutionalize much of the knowledge and know-how generated by their human capital. A list of such knowledge would include at least the following:

- Values and culture of the firm
- Mission, vision, objectives, and strategy of the firm
- Customer relationships and know-how about customers
- Technical knowledge and know-how
  - Commercializable innovations
    - Strategic innovations (part of the firm's strategic thrust)
    - Non-strategic innovations (available for out-licensing or other value-capturing process)
  - Other innovations that bring value to the firm
    - Innovations for internal operations (production/production processes)
    - Innovations that protect commercializable innovations

- Organization and structure of the firm
- Managerial methods
  - Decision processes
  - Databases
  - Procedures
- Work methods
- Information that provides access to company know-how and capabilities

Some of this knowledge and know-how is tacit and resides within the firm's human capital. The remainder, the portion that is codified, becomes the firm's intellectual assets.

CODIFIED KNOWLEDGE

Intellectual assets are the *codified* knowledge and know-how of the firm's human capital. Exhibit 9.1 shows the relationship

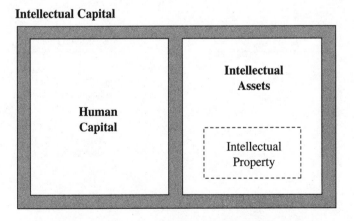

Exhibit 9.1   The Intellectual Capital of the Firm

Source: Patrick H. Sullivan, *Profiting from Intellectual Capital: Extracting Value from Innovation.* Copyright © 1998 by John Wiley & Sons, Inc. Reprinted by permission of John Wiley & Sons, Inc.

between intellectual capital, human capital, and intellectual assets.

Although the firm does not own its human capital, it does own the intellectual assets. Human capital, employees and stakeholders, may sever their relationship with the firm at any time. Employees may retire, resign, be laid off, or be terminated. Whatever their knowledge or know-how, regardless of whether they brought it when hired or learned it during their employ, it departs with them when they go. But any bits of knowledge that have become codified remain with and are the property of the firm. Codified bits of knowledge add to the firm's storehouse and stock of intellectual capital. In addition, once committed to media, an idea can be shared with others, discussed, improved, and expanded. It can be easily communicated to decision-makers, and actions can be taken or decisions made on its basis. In short, a codified bit of knowledge, an intellectual asset, can be leveraged by the firm, and leveragable intellectual assets are what knowledge companies seek to develop.

Intellectual assets are codified bits of knowledge of two types: commercializable and structural (see Exhibit 9.2).

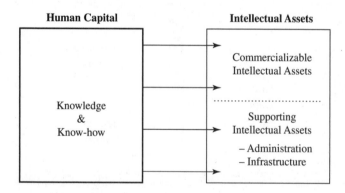

Exhibit 9.2   Intellectual Assets

COMMERCIALIZABLE INTELLECTUAL ASSETS

Commercializable intellectual assets are those that can be sold in the business or the technology marketplace. Examples of commercializable intellectual assets for business use include trademarks, names, products, product features, and manufacturing processes. There are two kinds of commercial intellectual assets, those that are legally protected and those that are not.

1. *Legally protected intellectual assets.* The portion of the intellectual assets that is legally protected is collectively referred to as the firm's intellectual property. IP may include patents, copyrights, trademarks, trade secrets, and semiconductor masks.

2. *Unprotected intellectual assets.* The unprotected and commercializable intellectual assets of the knowledge firm are usually the firm's innovations that are still undergoing further development.

Technical intellectual assets are bits of know-how that can be commercialized themselves or support another piece of commercialized technology. In technology companies the technical intellectual assets are of two kinds: design and operations.

1. *Design intellectual assets* are related to the firm's major activity, such as new production technologies or improved product features.

2. *Operations intellectual assets* are useful in the daily conduct of the firm's business, which for a manufacturing company might include manufacturing methods, processes, and procedures. For other companies these intellectual assets may be the documents, drawings, or otherwise codified bits of knowledge that define and guide the activities of employees. Documents that record operational activity are often of great commercial potential. For example, considerable business leverage may come from coordinating

159

the information contained in licensing agreements, confidential disclosure agreements, joint venture agreements, outsourcing contracts, and customer lists, documents that are otherwise not usually correlated.

INTELLECTUAL ASSETS AND STRUCTURAL CAPITAL

Many of the firm's intellectual assets become part of its structural capital, which is appropriate as they are part of the firm's infrastructure. Structural capital includes administrative and technical methods, processes, and procedures, as well as the firm's organizational structure—that is, the reporting relationships, and assignments of responsibility and authority of its human capital.

An earlier model of the knowledge firm showed intellectual capital and structural capital as related but separate from each other. In Exhibit 9.3 we can see that the two forms of capital actually merge with each other around the intellectual assets that are part of the firm's structural capital infrastructure.

As the firm grows and adds more physical assets, its structural capital grows as well. Likewise, over time the intellectual capital of the firm grows as it hires more employees (human capital) and the employees codify their ideas into intellectual capital. The structural capital actually grows as more and more infrastructure-related intellectual assets are generated and used by the firm. The firm's structural capital becomes one of two loci of the firm's history, culture, and values (the other, of course, is the employees themselves, the human capital).

Whether diagrammed as part of the intellectual capital or the structural capital, the growth in intellectual assets over time adds to the firm's stock of intellectual capital and provides more methods, processes, and procedures for leveraging the commercializable intellectual assets in the marketplace. These add to the firm's value. The degree to which the stock market

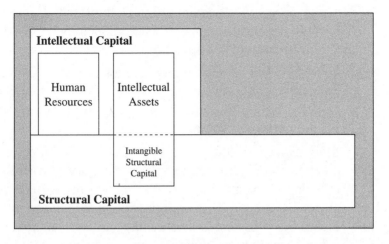

Exhibit 9.3   Model of a Knowledge Firm Showing Intangible Structural Capital

Source: Patrick H. Sullivan, *Profiting from Intellectual Capital: Extracting Value from Innovation.* Copyright © 1998 by John Wiley & Sons, Inc. Reprinted by permission of John Wiley & Sons, Inc.

sees or expects to see leveraging as adding to the firm's revenues is the degree to which the stock market will add a premium to the firm's stock price.

The structural intellectual assets that are not directly commercializable but that describe or define the ways in which the firm operates, include the following kinds of knowledge:

- *Organizational structure.* These are the roles, responsibilities, and hierarchical and financial relationships.
- *Customer capital.* Whereas the relationship portion of customer capital resides within the human capital of the firm, the portion of the company's information on customers that can be codified into databases or otherwise systematized is part of the firm's intangible structural capital.
- *Operational methods and procedures.* Documents that describe how the organization operates, whether in a business or a technical sense, are important components of the firm's structural capital.

- *Managerial methods and analyses.* Intellectual assets relating to the firm's managerial activities may be strategic, administrative, or collective:
  - *Strategic:* Intellectual assets categorized as strategic typically include the company's vision for the future, its strategy for getting there, and long-term plans for implementing the strategy.
  - *Administrative:* The bulk of the managerial intellectual assets are probably found in this category. Typically included in the administrative category are intellectual assets associated with administrative or managerial methods, processes, and procedures, as well as organizational structures, organization charts, job descriptions, and assignments of responsibility and authority.
  - *Collective:* Some of the firm's intellectual assets may describe or define the firm's collective ethos or way of doing business, including know-how and knowledge related to the culture and values of the firm.

Exhibit 9.4, an exploded view of a knowledge firm's intellectual assets, shows that the intellectual asset category of intel-

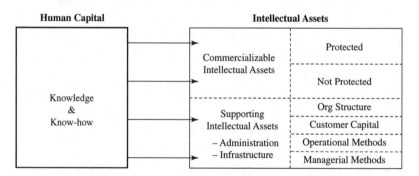

Exhibit 9.4   Intellectual Assets Component of Intellectual Capital

Source: Patrick H. Sullivan, *Profiting from Intellectual Capital: Extracting Value from Innovation.* Copyright © 1998 by John Wiley & Sons, Inc. Reprinted by permission of John Wiley & Sons, Inc.

lectual capital contains more than just commercializable assets (intellectual properties).

MANAGING INTELLECTUAL ASSETS

The management of intellectual assets builds upon the systems and methods firms put into place to manage their intellectual properties. An intellectual asset management system (IAMS) has all of the same components and elements of an intellectual property management system (IPMS) with two significant differences. First, the portfolio, heretofore one for each kind of IP, now contains additional portfolio sections for each new kind of intellectual assets. The selection of which intellectual assets to include in the IAMS depends, of course, on the company's context, vision, strategy, and roles for IC. Second, the competitive assessment function is more complex because the IA manager now seeks a broader range of intelligence information because of the broader range of internal information of interest.

One technology company's business strategy required that they obtain access to the technology of other companies whenever such technology was critical to their own future business opportunities. With this in mind, the intellectual asset manager created an internal program to provide the company's negotiating team with as much ammunition as possible for any discussions it might have with competing technology companies to access their technology. The IA manager gathered together all of his company's licenses (both in- and out-licenses), its confidential disclosure agreements, non-compete agreements, contracts with suppliers and vendors, contracts with the government, joint research agreements, professional services agreements, merger and acquisition agreements (both actual and potential), and divestiture agreements. Using these internal documents as the intellectual assets from which he could draw, whenever a technology competitor was identified as having a patented technology of interest, the IA manager would search his portfolio of intellectual assets to learn where and how the target company might be in violation of one or more agreements or stipulations. In this way, the IA manager was able to create a set of intellectual assets that were useful in supporting the firm's overall business strategy.

In the case of the second area of difference between IPMSs and IAMSs, competitive intelligence, the firm is interested in learning selected information about its innovation competitors. (Note: for many firms there is already a business intelligence function. Here we are discussing an intelligence function that focuses on firms who might be classified as innovation competitors, those that compete because they create innovations that are in the same area of interest as those of one's own firm. Most often innovation competitors are also business competitors, but this is not always the case. It may be that some of a firm's innovation competitors are actually in businesses in very different markets or even in different industries.)

Whereas in an IPMS, the competitive intelligence function may focus on obtaining information about a competitor's patent portfolio, or its IP strategy, in the case of an IAMS the competitive intelligence function may in addition obtain information about competitor licenses, business practices, or internal systems and methods involving innovation to name a few. The point here is that for an IAMS the competitive intelligence function is more expansive and is concerned with a wider range of intelligence information as is a system focused only on IP.

MEASURING AND VALUING
INTELLECTUAL ASSETS

Operational Value and the Knowledge Company

While the financial markets are interested in the current value of knowledge companies, the companies themselves are concerned about their future value. Knowledge companies generally manage their IC in order to create a future income stream and to support the strategy they have developed to achieve their vision. For this reason, the primary reference point for the measurement of the operational value/worth of intellectual capital is the firm's vision and strategy. The primary context for measuring value/worth is the values of the firm. Economic value/worth measurement may be done either qualitatively or quantitatively. Qualitative measures of economic value/worth describe the manner in which an intangible brings utility to the firm. Quantitative measures of value/worth define the amount of a stock or flow or the rate of change of a stock or flow. Many quantitative measures of intellectual capital use money as the primary dimension for measurement.

Measuring Operational Economic Value

Two monetary measures of value are price and cost. Price is the amount a purchaser is willing to pay in exchange for the utility received from an item. Cost is the amount of money required to produce an item. Both cost and price are considered to be direct (and quantitative) measures of value, but there are other, non-monetary or indirect measures of value as well.

Qualitative Measures of Value

Suppose a company, Acme Widget, wants to know the value of one of its patents. One way of exploring value would be to ask, "what value does this patent bring to the firm by its inclusion in the portfolio?" The answer may be qualitative. The value of this patent to the portfolio depends on several factors:

1. The intended use of the patent:
   - *Commercialization.* If this patent is in the portfolio to be commercialized, its value may be expressed as its usefulness to the firm in commercialization terms. For example, a patent that is by itself the complete technical basis for a business would be qualitatively more valuable than a patent that required other patented technologies to create a sufficient technical basis for a business.

- *Protection.* If this patent is in the portfolio to protect another patent that the firm does expect to commercialize, its value is related to the amount of protection it provides to the patent(s) it is included to protect.

- *Anti-competition.* If this patent is in the portfolio as an anti-competitive measure, it is there to provide:

  - *Blocking.* Denial of access by competitors to a predetermined field of technology

  - *Design freedom.* Freedom for the firm to continue conducting research and development in a particular field.

- *Litigation avoidance.* A patent may be in the portfolio to be used in bargaining with potential litigants in order to prevent a trial or arbitration.

2. The patent's ability to exclude others:

   - A patent may be able to exclude others from infringing on a firm's rights to practice R&D as well as to exclusively use the patented technology in the marketplace. Patents that can exclude virtually all potential infringers have high value for a firm. Patents with a limited ability to exclude others from practicing in a field have lower value.

3. The company's ability to detect infringement

   - The degree to which infringement of a patented technology can be detected is another measure of the value a patent may bring to its owner. It is difficult to detect infringement of a patented *process* because infringing applications are usually inside a machine or system. Infringement of *product* patents is often easier to detect because a product may usually be seen in the marketplace. Patents whose infringement is easy to detect are more valuable than those whose infringement is difficult to detect.

Quantitative Measures of Value

A range of quantitative measures may be used to measure the value of intellectual capital, both money-based and not. Things to be measured are often stocks (the total amount of something) or flows (the change or rate of change of something). Exhibit 9.5 shows examples of quantitative measures of intellectual capital value.

One final point concerning the quantification of value is the importance of the time dimension to value measurement. Some intellectual assets have current value to the firm, while others represent value to be realized sometime in the future. Intellectual capital management is the management of the firm's future. It largely deals with the processes for creating and commercializing innovations that will account for the firm's future income stream. Current intellectual capital, or the current stock of intellectual capital, is sometimes of interest to the financial markets. For this reason there are several efforts afoot to create a reliable set of methods for capitalizing this set of intangibles in the form of an intellectual capital balance sheet.

The measures used to value intellectual capital depend on the purpose of measuring. Measurements of the current stocks of intellectual capital are of interest outside the firm. Of interest inside the firm are those measures that tell one of two things: First, are the innovations being developed proceeding as planned? and, second, what can each innovation be expected to produce in the form of an income stream, and what is the net present value of that income stream?

QUANTIFYING VALUE IN MONETARY TERMS

A range of methods is available for quantifying value in terms of money. The method selected depends on the reasons the valuation is to be made and the degree of precision required. The most com-

Identification	Management	Extraction	Alignment and Systemization

• Definition of Assets:
  – Number
  – Costs to Date
  – Forecast Costs
  – Subject/Techn.
  – Age
  – Remaining Life
  – Value Category
  – Rate of Addition
  – Rate of Deletion
• Categorization of Assets:
  – Number of Categories
  – Number of IA's in Category
  – Number or % not in Category
  – Alignment with Vision
	• General:
	  – Number of Evals/Unit Time
	  – Number of Techniques Avail.
	  – Number of Staff
	  – Alignment with Vision
	  – Skill Level of Staff
	  – Number of Recc's Made
	  – Number of Recc's Implemented
	  – Quality of Evals
	  – Backlog
		• For each:
		  – Number of Innovations
		  – $ Invested
		  – $ Received
		  – Forecast Income
		  – Alignment with Vision
			• Information Systems:
			  – % Coverage
			  – % Complete
			  – Accessibility
			  – Completeness
			  – Rate of Usage
			  – Alignment
			• Decision Systems:
			  – Age
			  – Coverage
			  – Purpose
			  – Comprehensiveness
			  – Connectivity
			  – Alignment
			• Managerial Systems
			  – Satisfaction
			  – Rate of Usage

Exhibit 9.5 Examples of Quantitative Measures of Value

mon reasons for a knowledge company to produce a money-based valuation of an intangible asset are: litigation; tax-related transactions; joint ventures; intracompany transfers; business decision-making; out-licensing/sale; in-licensing/purchase; R&D investment; portfolio management; in-kind contributions; exploitation potential; and initial estimate of value.

The precision required of a valuation may be determined by the relative importance of the result as well as the degree of scrutiny to which valuation will be subjected. The amount of precision determines the amount of effort and resources expended on answering the question: How much is it worth (what is its dollar value)? Exhibit 9.6 suggests a relationship between the reason for valuing, the expected degree of scrutiny, and the level of effort required to produce a valuation.

Valuation Methods

Value is quantified in monetary terms through one of the three classic methods:

Reason for Valuation	Expected Degree of Scrutiny	Level of Effort Required
Litigation	Very High	High
Tax-related Transactions	High	High
Joint Ventures	High	High
Intracompany Transfers	High	High
Business Decision-making	Medium	Medium
Licensing	Medium	Medium
In-Kind Contributions	Medium	Medium
R&D Investment	Medium	Medium
Portfolio Management	Medium	Medium
Exploitation Potential	Medium	Medium
Initial Estimate	Low	Low

Exhibit 9.6   Relationship between Circumstance, Scrutiny, and Valuation Effort

- *Market method.* This method, probably the top choice of economists, uses the market price agreed upon by willing buyer and seller as the best dollar measure of utility.
- *Income method.* This method, usually used when there is not a market price available, involves calculating the future streams of income and cost and then discounting their sum back to present value.
- *Cost method.* Perhaps the least preferred by economists, the cost method calculates the costs required to duplicate (create an exact copy of) or replicate (to create the functional equivalent of) an intangible.

Exhibit 9.7 lists some of the uses of these money-based valuation methods.

A comparison of Exhibits 9.6 and 9.7 reveals that valuation requires a high level of training and experience.

SUMMARY

The intellectual assets of a firm, its codified (and unprotected) information that can be converted into profits, is well-defined. Intellectual assets are of many kinds and may be categorized and sub-categorized under a range of headings. Most of the firm's intellectual assets are a part of its intellectual capital, yet some of these intangibles may find their way into an intangible element of the firm's structural capital. Intellectual assets are systematized and managed very similarly to the firm's intellectual property. Firms graduating from an intellectual property management system to an intellectual asset management system find two elements of increased complexity: the number and kinds of portfolios of assets to be managed and the increased amount and kind of information of interest about innovation competitors. Finally, measurement and valuation of intellectual assets have been discussed and ideas about methods and approaches have been listed.

Method	Description	Advantages	Disadvantages	When Used
Market (classic)	• The economist's basic valuation method	• Best match with Economist's definition of value	• Difficult to find comparable IPs	• Litigation • Licensing Transaction
Income (classic)	• A basic technique on which many variations are based	• Quantities cost and income streams. • Considered best alternative if market approach is unavailable	• Difficult for layman to calculate	• Litigation
Cost (classic)	• A calculation of the cost to replicate or reproduce	• A third approach used when the market income approach is not available • Good method for brand-new technology	• No measure of utility or market value • Overhead allocations difficult to make/justify	• Litigation
Technology Factor	• Devised by Dow, a good method for internal valuation	• Builds political consensus • Methodical/systematic • Good workbook	• Requires assembly of many people • Many assumptions underlying method • Does not necessarily apply to companies other than DOW	• For internal use only
Probability-Adjusted Expected Value	• Method for valuation under uncertainty	• Allows for quantification of elements of risk • Models the development process	• Difficult for laymen to calculate • Can be costly if done to meet high precision standards	• Where "strategicness" is important

Exhibit 9.7   Example Valuation Methods

(*Continues*)

Method	Description	Advantages	Disadvantages	When Used
Risk/Hurdle Rate	• Financially focused method	• Quantifies risk • Mathematical analysis	• Intensive calculation • Not for the faint-at-heart	• Financial Investment
Return on Sales	• A calculation of royalty based on net sales	• Quick • Take advantage of industry norms	• Difficult to allocate profits between two parties • Value could be different from one company to another • Requires agreed sales forecasts	• N/A
Sullivan's Method	• A quick method with a basis in theory *and* a coupling with judgment	• Quick • Based on business knowledge • Order-of-magnitude results	• Accurate to ±25% • Requires some market knowledge • Uses average exhibits	• Initial Estimate
Make Me an Offer	• Just what it says	• Good approach when *no* valuation information is available	• Leaves money on the table	• All circumstances
25% Rule	• A rule of thumb	• Simple • Provides an agreed (if not accurate) value • Used only when nothing else is available	• No basis in theory • Not necessarily accurate or representative	• Initial Estimate

Exhibit 9.7 (*Continued*)

10

Extracting Value
from Human Capital
(Basic Concepts)

The second dimension of the IC framework contains the
non-accounting models of a knowledge firm. One of the
core pieces of those models is the intellectual capital of the firm.
The concepts surrounding intellectual capital and IC management have evolved along two paths: a knowledge-related path
and dollar-related path. These have led to two different ways
of managing intellectual capital: through knowledge and
learning activities (value creation) and through business and
financial activities (value extraction); see Exhibit 10.1. The language spoken by people in the two areas is different; their values and objectives are different; they are engaged in different
kinds of activity; and they read different kinds of professional
literature.

The activities associated with *creating new knowledge*
(increasingly called value-creation activities) are based on the
methods and literature in the fields of education, psychology,
sociology, and religion. Activities in this area are heavily
focused on the human capital component of IC, the firm's
employees. Value-creation activities concern methods for

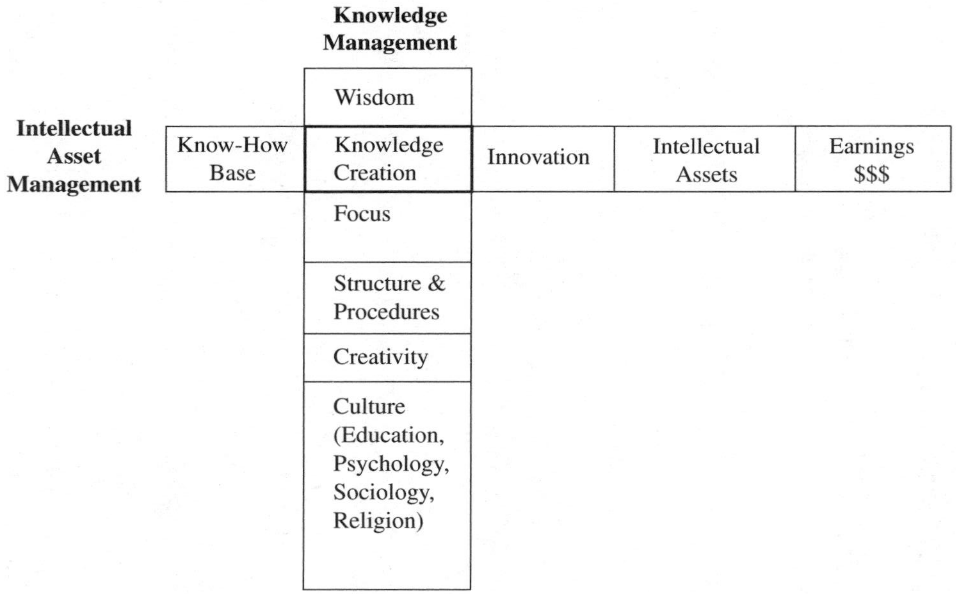

Knowledge Management

	Wisdom			
Know-How Base	Knowledge Creation	Innovation	Intellectual Assets	Earnings $$$
	Focus			
	Structure & Procedures			
	Creativity			
	Culture (Education, Psychology, Sociology, Religion)			

Intellectual Asset Management

Exhibit 10.1 Intersection of Knowledge Management and Intellectual Asset Management

Source: Patrick H. Sullivan, *Profiting from Intellectual Capital: Extracting Value from Innovation.* Copyright © 1998 by John Wiley & Sons, Inc. Reprinted by permission of John Wiley & Sons, Inc.

improving innovation, new organizational forms, the values and culture of the organization, and the relationships between and among the individuals and groups in the organization. Also included here are the activities associated with information-sharing systems, often called knowledge-management systems.

The activities of the resource-based view of the firm (the value-extraction side of intellectual capital management) are based on the methods and literature of economics, law, business, finance, and accounting. These activities are heavily focused on the documents and drawings that embody the firm's innovations. Ideally, these documents and drawings are converted into products and services and then into operational businesses that produce profits for the firm.

This chapter will provide background and understanding so that value extractors can differentiate between tacit and explicit knowledge. While tacit knowledge is the basis for the firm's intellectual capital, explicit, codified knowledge (intellectual assets) is often easier to use for developing profits.

KNOWLEDGE AND INTELLECTUAL CAPITAL

Many people understand tacit knowledge and intellectual capital to be the same thing. People with this perspective view knowledge as the basis on which a company builds its future. Often their focus is on creating new or more focused knowledge. Knowledge is the fundamental driver of intellectual capital; it comes in many forms and concerns many topics of interest to the corporation. A company's administrative knowledge comprises procedures, methods, and decision processes necessary for the management of the firm. A firm that understands its value-added activities can ensure that its procedures are efficient, effective, and timely. Probably the most significant of all firm knowledge is knowledge that adds value for the firm's customers.

The firm may acquire knowledge, tacit information that resides inside employees' heads, by any number of means. Some firms seek people with specific knowledge and offer them attractive salaries to contribute their expertise to the knowledge bank of the firm. Other firms purchase companies that already possess the knowledge they want to acquire. Still others rent it, by licensing in the rights to use the needed knowledge or create the knowledge themselves by developing methods and processes that encourage creativity and innovation among their employees.

Knowledge is more than the sum of bits of data and information. Merely converting data and information from research reports and computers into tacit information does not create knowledge. Knowledge creation is often described as proceeding in steps: from *data* to *information* to *knowledge* to *wisdom*. The progression suggests that information can be created from data, that information that is assimilated becomes tacit knowledge, and that the accumulation of knowledge is wisdom.

Karl-Eric Sveiby disputes the accuracy of this description. Sveiby, in a conversation with the author, stated "although it is not unreasonable to say that data may be aggregated to create information, it is unreasonable to suggest that the process of converting information into knowledge is as uncomplicated as the simple progression of steps implies."

The process of transferring explicit information from a printed piece of paper to one's head is called learning. *But information acquired in this way is not knowledge*. Only when bits of learned information are *used* do they become knowledge. Converting memorized information into knowledge may be as simple as learning addition and subtraction and then using that information to calculate whether one has enough money to make a purchase.

Wisdom, of course, involves not only accumulating knowledge, but also possessing a set of ethics and a sense of morality about its use.

A KNOWLEDGE-BASED MODEL OF INTELLECTUAL CAPITAL

The most popular model of intellectual capital from the human capital perspective has evolved from the independent work of two of the thought leaders on knowledge and human capital. Karl-Eric Sveiby and Hubert St. Onge, although working independently, have together contributed to this model of the tacit portion of the firm's intellectual capital, seen in Exhibit 10.2.

St. Onge defines intellectual capital as the sum of employee capital, organizational capital, and external relationship capital:

1. *Employee capital* is the capability of individual employees to provide solutions to customers.
2. *Organizational capital* is the organization's ability to meet market requirements.
3. *External relationships* represent the depth (penetration), width (coverage), attachment (loyalty), and profitability of the company's franchise.

This model focuses on the organization's tacit knowledge and relationships. It illustrates that the human capital of the

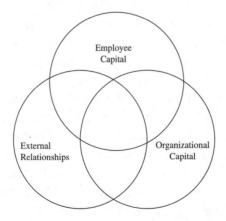

Exhibit 10.2   A Knowledge-Based View of Intellectual Capital

firm has individual as well as collective knowledge, know-how, and relationships. The firm's ability to focus this individual and collective set of capabilities on customer problems allows it to create value for its customers. The strength of this model is its focus on improving the effort and output of the firm's employees, while its weakness is its lack of financial or economic dimensions. The knowledge-based model of IC is a significant contribution to the evolution of the management of *tacit* intellectual capital within the firm.

THE RELATIVE IMPORTANCE
OF DIFFERENT KINDS OF KNOWLEDGE

Not all knowledge has equal value. The value of knowledge depends upon a range of factors that are unique to each company. The degree to which a piece of knowledge relates to the company's operations, its strategy or tactics, or its focus determines the value that that piece of knowledge has to a firm. A bit of knowledge may have a different degree of importance and value in one firm than in another. Likewise, not all knowledge within a firm can be converted into profits, and among the convertible portions some is more convertible than others. For example, suppose we have two companies that manufacture widgets: Acme Widget and Omega Widget. Suppose that Acme Widget buys the raw materials, makes all widget components itself, and then assembles its widgets from the components it manufactures. Omega Widget, on the other hand, purchases widget components from outside suppliers and then assembles its widgets from the purchased components. Knowledge about assembly has value to both companies, whereas knowledge about component manufacture only has value to Acme Widget, the component manufacturer.

Some knowledge is worth more to the corporation than other knowledge. Usually we think of businesses in functional terms—that is, as a series of activities or functions which, when combined, constitute the whole firm. This view arose almost a century ago in the waning days of the industrial era when manufacturing was king. By that time it had become clear that profits were made by manufacturing physical products cheaply and efficiently. Efficiency meant not only performing individual tasks in a cost-effective manner but also organizing the company itself in ways that promoted an effective and low-cost set of internal processes. In this kind of organization the functions to be performed are used as a basis for the organizational structure. This view sees firms as a combination of staff and line functions whose activities are carefully orchestrated so that together they constitute a functioning whole. Typical line functions are R&D, design, manufacturing, warehousing, and transportation. Staff functions may be related to legal issues, accounting, human resources, and information systems.

The functional view is but one of several traditional frameworks for viewing businesses, among them the accounting framework, according to which businesses are viewed as balance sheets or stacks of assets and liabilities, and the operating perspective, which views companies as sets of expenditure categories: sales and marketing, rent, legal and accounting, cost of goods sold, taxes, etc.

These traditional frameworks for viewing the firm, each helpful in its own way, proved not to be useful to firms that wanted to put their management energies into improving value for their customers. For this purpose a new framework was developed around the concept of adding value. The value-added framework is useful for firms engaged in knowledge activities because it allows them to determine which kind of knowledge is important (see Exhibit 10.3).

VALUE-ADDED KNOWLEDGE

The value-added framework is based on the concept that firms add value to physical or intangible assets and sell this added

Valued-Added Knowledge	Very valuable to the firm. Often provides unique capabilities that differentiate the firm from competitors.
Direct Support Knowledge	Valuable knowledge for the firm. Sometimes provides differentiation from competition.
Indirect Support Knowledge	Useful knowledge for the firm. Maintains infrastructure so that firm may pursue its value-added activity.

Exhibit 10.3   Types of Knowledge from a Value-Added Perspective

value to their customers. Such firms need to determine exactly what value they are adding (and to what are they adding it). Firms that assemble components into finished products add value through the assembly process. Other firms take raw materials, manufacture components from these raw materials, and then assemble them into finished products. This kind of firm adds value through the creation of the components and through their assembly into a finished product.

Value-added knowledge relates directly to the innovations and their product features or functions. It might be knowledge about manufacturing or distribution capabilities or about customers and their requirements. Quite often this kind of knowledge provides a firm with a unique capability that competitors lack.

Rockwell International, for example, creates value in its semiconductor division by integrating the ideas and innovations of others into their own products. Other companies, such as IBM, excel at creating new innovations and then using them in products as well as in the manufacturing process to create products their customers value.

Companies may use the value-added concept to help them identify the portion of their knowledge that is of particular value. What are the raw materials used by the firm (tangible or intangible, physical or intellectual)? How does the firm add value to these materials?

Value-added organizations may be thought of as performing three kinds of activity: those that add value to a product or service, that directly support the value-added activity, and that indirectly support the value-added activity.

DIRECT-SUPPORT KNOWLEDGE

Knowledge that directly supports the firm's value-added activity, while valuable to the firm, may be less crucial than the value-added knowledge described above. This knowledge includes administrative knowledge, company plans, methods, and procedures.

INDIRECT-SUPPORT KNOWLEDGE

This type of knowledge supports the firm's infrastructure. It includes all of the generic functions and work that must be accomplished in order to provide the "beans and bullets" necessary to produce the profit-generating products and innovations of the firm. Activities in this area include accounting, janitorial services, financial services, information systems, and corporate services.

HOW KNOWLEDGE IS USED

Knowledge that has strategic uses may have more value for companies than knowledge that has support uses. Equally, knowledge that has tactical uses may have great value in the short term but not necessarily in the long term.

From the Greek *strategos,* meaning "the work of the generals," strategy is concerned with meeting the fundamental long-term objectives of the firm. A strategy is often the set of decisions and activities involved with moving the firm from its current position toward the achievement of its long-term vision. Strategy is often contrasted with tactics. In military terms, strategy involves activities associated with winning a war; tactics concerns activities associated with winning a battle. Necessarily, strategy has a longer time perspective and is concerned with larger and more fundamental goals. Tactics must succeed in the short term in order for the strategy to succeed in the long term.

Other activities of the firm may be neither strategic nor tactical. They fall under the broad heading of support activities, which include the supply, logistics, and staff work underlying all firm activity, whether strategic or tactical (see Exhibit 10.4).

Strategic Knowledge	• Knowledge involves long-term positioning or value to the firm • Knowledge relates to corporate vision or strategies of that achievement
Tactical Knowledge	• Knowledge involves short-term positioning or value • Knowledge relates to markets, competitors, and suppliers and/or near-term activities elsewhere
Support Knowledge	• Knowledge involves internal operation or activities facilitation, strategic or tactical activity • Knowledge relates to infrastructure activities

Exhibit 10.4   Types of Knowledge from a Strategic Perspective

Companies that derive their strategic advantage from the creation of unique combinations of tangible and intangible assets may place a higher priority on internally focused knowledge. Companies that develop a strategic advantage by finding and filling market niches may find that externally focused knowledge has great importance or value.

In the final analysis, knowledge that is unique to a firm, that provides it with opportunities to develop unique combinations of assets (intangible and tangible), is more valuable than generic knowledge that can be accessed widely in the marketplace. Knowledge or innovations that firms develop and use in the creation of new or additional value is particularly valuable. Exhibit 10.5 summarizes the major dimensions within which firms may describe and define their knowledge.

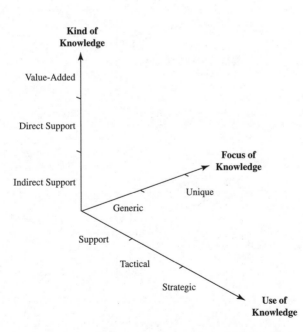

Exhibit 10.5   Some Major Dimensions of Knowledge

183

VALUE CREATION AND VALUE EXTRACTION

Value creation and value extraction are the two activities associated with intellectual capital. Value creation involves the creation of new knowledge and its dissemination. Exhibit 10.6 describes some of the major differences between the two activities.

Successful companies employ a set of intertwined and interacting management tools and capabilities. Companies that want to increase their odds of successfully developing profits from their hidden capital need to understand their own capabilities, the power of the tools available to them, and to ensure that both are in place and in working order. The tools and capabilities fall into three categories: (1) direction and context for the firm; (2) organizational capabilities (background and foreground); and (3) value-extraction chains.

	Value Creation	Value Extraction
Purpose	To increase employee knowledge in order to create new or improved innovations for commercialization	To leverage company innovations in order to maximize profits and/or improve strategic position
IC Focus	Human capital (employees)	Intellectual assets (paper)
Activities	Knowledge creation Knowledge sharing Learning Organizational dynamics Information technology	Definition/measurement Overseeing innovation process Generation and maintenance of IA Competitive assessment Enforcement Conversion to profits
Conceptual Underpinnings	Psychology Education Sociology Religion	Economics Finance Law Strategy

Exhibit 10.6   Value Creation and Value Extraction

BALANCING VALUE-CREATION
AND VALUE-EXTRACTION ACTIVITIES

Corporations around the world are striving to create new knowledge, and from that, new innovations that they can convert into value. This focus on knowledge is entirely appropriate and well placed. Profit-seeking businesses, however, should ask themselves whether the amount of value being created is matched by an appropriately sized capability to *realize* the value. In other words, for each innovation, as well as for each kind of value the firm wishes to realize from its IC, are there resources, activities, and people in place to extract the value (either in the form of cash or in strategic positioning)?

Some companies lose sight of the end goal of creating such corporate knowledge, which is to convert it to stakeholder value. An often-asked question is whether it is more important for knowledge companies to create new innovations and ideas or to focus on extracting the value from those they already have in hand. The answer, of course, is that it depends. Companies with a surfeit of innovations need to sift through them and filter out only the best and most interesting innovations for investment. Once this is done, their investment dollars might best be put into the creation of more and better capabilities to extract greater amounts of value from their intellectual assets.

Likewise, firms without enough innovations or creative ideas to commercialize need to spend their internal investment dollars on becoming more creative.

On the spectrum of activity from value creation to value extraction the successful knowledge firm will find an equilibrium position. The optimum balance between creation and extraction is for the firm to create ideas at a pace that is compatible with the pace at which they can be screened and their value extracted.

In firms with a balanced approach to intellectual capital management, the two sets of activities are in proportion. Most firms pursue one or the other activity strongly and believe that their approach is adequate if not optimal. It has been my experience that firms spend more time, energy, and resources on value creation than on value extraction. Firms that overdo creation are frequently unable to see that their IC activities are disproportionate.

Indeed, it may be helpful for firms to visualize themselves on a two-by-two diagram, with value creation on one axis and value extraction on the other. Such a measuring device might look like Exhibit 10.7.

- *Value-creation activity is high (quadrants I and IV).* Companies in this position may have an abundance of innovations and ideas. Such companies should screen their innovations to identify the ones that make the most sense to invest in and pursue to development.

- *Value-creation activity is low (quadrants II and III).* Companies in this position should encourage their staffs to develop more new ideas and products. Such companies may also look outside the firm for ideas and innovations through in-licensing or by hiring new employees.

- *Value-extraction activity is high (quadrants III and IV).* Companies in this position may have a surfeit of technolo-

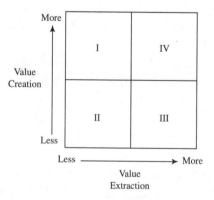

Exhibit 10.7   Value Creation—Value Extraction Matrix

gies in the value-extraction pipeline. Such companies usually have established a variety of methods for extracting value. They are typically well staffed for value extraction, with a variety of offices that perform related but different responsibilities, including licensing, pursuing joint ventures and strategic alliances, and handling donation and tax activities.

- *Value-extraction activity is low (quadrants I and II).* Companies in this position typically invest only a small amount of their human resources in value extraction. They tend to focus their value-extraction activity in the Intellectual Property department and soon the legal staff is overbooked with work. In addition to all of the activities associated with interacting with inventors, determining which inventions are patentable, drafting and reviewing patents, and preparing and prosecuting patent filings, the staff will also be asked to handle licenses, contracts, joint ventures, and strategic alliances. Low value-extraction companies focus their value-extraction activities on the business divisions and main products and services of the firm. Little attention is given to other forms of value extraction, and only relatively small amounts of value are extracted from the firm's intellectual assets.

Companies in quadrant I are sub-optimizing their investment in knowledge-creation processes and systems. Many companies with hundreds or thousands of inventions and patents do not have the intellectual asset management (IAM) systems in place to extract value from the "gems" while minimizing the costs associated with the duds. The managers of companies in this quadrant often need to be persuaded to invest in such systems. Benchmarking studies that highlight what competitors are doing and identify best practices in value extraction can be helpful. Investing carefully in evaluating the revenue potential of languishing intellectual assets can help focus internal attention on the opportunities that may exist.

Companies in quadrant II have not created the processes and systems to create knowledge or to convert knowledge into shareholder value. The challenge for these companies is to educate employees about how knowledge is created. Typically the managers of companies in quadrant II have not yet understood the competitive implications of the knowledge revolution and are still operating under the old-fashioned industrial paradigm.

Companies in quadrant III have succeeded in creating an environment that fosters the extraction of value from their knowledge but have failed to create an environment in which knowledge will be routinely created and evaluated for commercialization and profits. Benchmarking studies and best-practice reviews that demonstrate how others are creating shareholder value can be helpful. An examination of how the investment community reacts to companies in quadrant IV could prove enlightening to managers.

Companies in quadrant IV have it all. The challenge for the management of such companies is to ensure that they have the capabilities to sustain such performance. An IC audit should be considered.

A company that assesses its relative strengths in value creation and value extraction will be able to determine how it should reshape its intellectual capital resources to more effectively support its business strategy and tactics. A simple matrix that describes the firm's value-creation and value-extraction positions along with recommended courses of action is a useful tool when making an IC position evaluation.

SUMMARY

The human capital of a knowledge firm is one of its most important assets. Managing the human capital in knowledge firms is more challenging than for non-knowledge firms because of the need to both create and extract value from this important element of intellectual capital. Understanding the difference between value creation activities and value extraction activities is an important step in understanding human capital (HC) management. Equally, understanding the different roles that HC may play depending upon the kind of knowledge company being managed is required in order to better manage both the value creation and value extraction activities of the human capital. Determining whether there is a balance between value creation and value extraction activities is often difficult to know. Some of the perspectives developed in this chapter should be a helpful foundation in understanding how to better focus the firm's human capital toward a most productive set of activities.

11

Extracting Value
from Human Capital
(Advanced Concepts)

M ost companies are not sufficiently aware of the dimensions of knowledge (see Exhibit 10.5) or of the differences between value creation and value extraction activities (see Exhibit 10.6) to be able to focus their human capital management energies on the greatest benefit for the firm. Human resources policies as well as management activities often treat all employees alike, when a view of the firm from the IC perspective suggests that not only are some employees more valuable than others, but they need to be directed, managed, and nurtured differently. This view is in opposition to the American egalitarian philosophy that says that, with the exception of compensation, all employees should be *treated* equally. In America, by law as well as by practice, usually all employees have the same, or strikingly similar, packages of benefits, number of holidays, number of vacation days, etc. Equally, it is often the case that incentive programs are often the same, if not similar, differing primarily to adapt to hourly vs. salaried pay plans.

In contrast with this nationalistic view, the intellectual capital perspective suggests that all employees are *not* the same and that certain employees, because of their ability to create the future of the firm, probably should be managed, compensated, and treated very differently from the others. In this chapter we will discuss management of the firm's human capital from a value extraction perspective.

Recently Sweden's Skandia, the insurance company that identified intellectual capital as its own core resource, announced that it will provide "intellectual capital insurance." The idea is that Skandia will identify the key pieces of a customer firm's intellectual capital (what we call the "core" human capital) and insure against that intellectual capital being lost to the customer firm. Once a policy has been agreed upon, Skandia develops programs and incentives to ensure that key people have every reason to remain with the firm, rather than be lured away to greener pastures. Further, if despite Skandia's efforts one of the core employees leaves, Skandia is obligated to find and hire a replacement with the same level of knowledge and skills as the person who left.

This chapter will discuss management of the firm's *core* human capital and how they may be best employed. Issues surrounding the firm's core human capital and the effect of different managerial styles and organizational structures on the output of the human capital will also be addressed.

CORE HUMAN CAPITAL

At the beginning of this book we defined intellectual capital as knowledge that can be converted into profit. We also said that intellectual capital has two major components: human capital and intellectual assets. Because it is now generally accepted that the term human capital refers to all of the firm's employees, we must find a way to differentiate any special set of employees from the others. The largest grouping of the firm's human capital is *not* core. The second, smaller, set of employees, however, creates the innovations that are converted into profits making them significantly different from the rest of the employees.

192

Because the ideas and innovations of this select group forms the basis for the firm's products or services and their creativity allows the firm to differentiate itself from its competitors, these employees create the firm's future, and are the *core* human capital of the firm.

CREATIVITY VS. PRODUCTIVITY

When viewing human capital from the value extraction perspective, there are two very different areas of focus for human capital. The selection of one over the other depends upon the kind of *firm* with which the human capital is associated. Intellectual capital firms may be divided into four different kinds, each with a unique set of requirements for intellectual capital management systems:

- *Product companies* are those whose primary value-added activity is the production of a product. Their focus is on product technologies, typically on product features as a way of differentiating themselves in the marketplace.

- *Process companies* are those that use a process to handle physical materials, such as refineries, manufacturers, and distributors. For all such companies, the primary business goal is to reduce the processing costs and increase the quality as well as the volume of output.

- *Service companies (continuous service)* are companies such as the telephone and utility companies that expend resources to create a network for the distribution of services; they utilize their intellectual capital to create and market an ever-broader set of services to customers, which they deliver through the network. The focus of most of their intellectual capital is on developing and marketing new services. They focus the remainder of their human capital on creating, improving, or maintaining the capability of their network, because the network is the device through which the firm's products or services are sold and delivered.

- *Service companies (discrete service)* offer services one at a time. These companies sell the knowledge of their human capital directly, for example, law firms, medical doctors, consulting firms, accounting firms, and others that commercialize the knowledge of their well-trained human capital.

As Exhibit 11.1 shows, these companies use their intellectual capital differently. They use different intellectual capital management systems and have different degrees of interest in the tactical and strategic uses of their intellectual capital. Not all aspects of the intellectual capital management perspective are appropriate for all knowledge firms. The same can be said for the *human capital* component of their intellectual capital, so each company must assess for itself the benefits and focus it selects for its human capital.

As Exhibit 11.1 also shows, not all knowledge companies have the same relative amount or kind of intellectual capital or focus for ICM. In addition, the table shows two different kinds of emphasis for the firm's human capital: creativity and productivity.

FOCUS FOR HUMAN CAPITAL

Firms place two different kinds of emphasis on their human capital. Which emphasis applies to a firm depends upon which kind of firm it is. When the human capital is expected to create new innovations and to convert them to intellectual assets in order for them to be commercialized, the human capital emphasis is twofold: creativity is most important, with productivity second. For discrete service firms, where the knowledge of the human capital is commercialized directly (typically paid for by the hour) the emphasis is on productivity first, with creativity second.

Company Type	Process Emphasis	Product Emphasis	Continuous Service Provided	Discrete Service Provided
Examples	Refinery Company, Oil & Gas Pipeline	Automobile Companies, Computer Companies	Electric & Gas Utilities, Telephone Companies, Banks, Insurance Companies	Law Firms, Consulting Firms, Accounting Firms
Intellectual Property	A Large Amount	A Large Amount	A Smaller Amount	Very Small Amount
Intellectual Assets	A Large Amount	A Large Amount	A Large Amount	A Small Amount
Human Capital	Focused on Technology	Focused on Technology	Focused on Products & Services as well as on technology	Focused on Services
HC Emphasis	Creativity	Creativity	Creativity	Productivity
ICM Focus	Tactical & Strategic	Tactical & Strategic	Tactical & Strategic	Tactical

Exhibit 11.1   Intellectual Capital and Human Capital by Company Type

The Creativity Focus for Human Capital

When the knowledge of the firm's human capital is to be codified for subsequent commercialization, the primary objective of the human capital is to maximize the number and quality of innovations. For three of the four company types, the human capital's focus is on creativity and all of the organizational elements that surround it. Organizations with this human capital focus are concerned about expanding their knowledge. They typically seek organizational forms and physical environments that encourage creativity as well as corporate cultures that value openness and sharing. Xerox's research center in Palo Alto, California was constructed with creativity in mind. Virtually all offices have white boards on the wall and many conference rooms have floor-to-ceiling whiteboards, to encourage people to jot down their ideas or to graphically illustrate an idea that has come up in a meeting. Some of the conference rooms have beanbag chairs and are otherwise furnished in a relaxing manner designed to put the occupants in a creative mood.

For companies with this focus, skilled and innovative human capital may not be easily obtained in the marketplace and must, of necessity, be developed internally. These companies typically have significant programs that encourage innovation as well as programs to inculcate in new employees the firm's culture and values regarding innovation. Maximizing value extraction for such firms involves maximizing the creativity of their human capital.

The task facing managers in companies that must codify the innovations of their human capital in order to better leverage it, is threefold: create an innovation-enhancing environment, focus creative energies onto innovations that align with the company's vision and strategy, and codify the most valuable ideas and innovations.

Creating an innovation-enhancing environment involves a range of activities designed to encourage innovative thought and knowledge sharing. These activities often involve reducing the barriers to innovation and codification more than they involve creating new programs or activities to encourage them. Management of activities in this realm centers on relationships, organizational structure, incentives and rewards, and alignment with strategy. Interestingly, the more managers are able to establish an environment that reduces the barriers created by awkward or inappropriate relationships and structure, the less they need to worry about creating new programs involving incentives, rewards, and alignment. The less the environment is based on supportive and empowering relationships and structures, the more reliance there must be on incentives and alignment. Managers who want to promote an innovation-enhancing environment must encourage employees to be eager to innovate and codify their innovations. Management style can have a dramatic effect on employee willingness to innovate, as can be seen in the following descriptions of various management styles.

Authoritarian Management Style

Consider the relationship between management style, organization structure, and employee innovation. A simple diagram shown in Exhibit 11.2 illustrates this point. When management

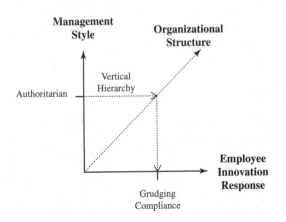

Exhibit 11.2   First-Level Relationship and Organizational Linkages

197

is authoritarian and directive, the structure of the organization is usually hierarchical, with communications flowing up and down within organizational silos. In organizations such as these, the manager or company executive issues orders or directives down through the chain of command. Employees at lower levels of the chain receive these orders and respond. This environment results in an employee attitude of grudging acceptance. Employees with this attitude are typically not especially innovative or interested in sharing their knowledge with others. They see management as having the company's interests at heart, not the employee's. For this reason, employees often guard their knowledge closely, only grudgingly sharing with others. After all, their knowledge may become a useful bargaining chip should they ever find themselves in a dispute with their authoritarian managers.

The authoritarian style of management, patterned after the paternal model of a family, supposes that the executive knows best. His or her role is to give directions to subordinates which they are expected to carry out without questioning the executive's authority. Employees who find themselves involved in companies espousing this model often feel exploited by the company and its management. They see that the company is using their ideas and innovations to create corporate wealth and that all the employee receives for the innovation is his or her wage. Companies using this style often find that incentives or rewards for performance are necessary.

Collegial Management Style

When management evolves to a more participative style, often called the collegial model of management, employees are consulted before they are directed to accomplish an assignment or task. Here employees have some means for tailoring or shaping their own activities or those of the group. This style of management is often found in organizations where the members are highly educated or trained and each has a self-view that includes a high degree of faith in one's own knowledge and skills and a relatively low degree of faith that "the boss is always right." Organizations espousing the collegial model of management often include university faculty departments, medical departments in hospitals, and political parties. Here all members of the organization view themselves as equals. The organization leader is someone who has agreed to take on the undesirable (and sometimes low-status) task of administering the organization. While day-to-day matters are left to the leader to decide and implement, all significant decisions are made by agreement with all members of the organization. This model is often characterized by the phrase: "come, let us reason together!" In this model, the leader has less power and authority than in the authoritarian model. The interests of individual organization members may or may not be consistent with the interests of the organization. In this model, the organizational structure is still hierarchical (although with fewer layers and levels than in the authoritarian model). When the organization asks something of the employees (even in a collegial manner) the individual has some influence on the kind of response they might be able to make. Nevertheless, many organizational theorists see the collegial model as nothing more than a kinder and gentler version of the authoritarian model. See Exhibit 11.3 for a comparison of the two management styles.

Equality Management Style

In this type of management, all members of the organization are considered to be of equal status. Each person in the organization has an equal ownership stake and is considered an expert in whatever their job involves. A classic example of this model of management is NASA's space flight crews. Each member of the crew is a highly intelligent and highly trained professional. Each of them could qualify as the leader, yet only one is so named. Each person functions well in his or her assignment, providing the others with information or services as required by

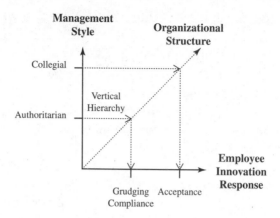

Exhibit 11.3   Second-Level Relationship and Organizational Linkages

the mission profile. Each participates fully in all major decisions made aboard the spacecraft; all have the same interest: to complete their mission and safely return to earth. In this model the organizational structure is flat. The organization continues to have leaders, although their role is in name only. There are no levels and there is no one person fully in charge. The organizational structure looks more like a fishing net than it does the old-fashioned boxes and lines type of chart. Individuals react, respond, and interact with one another eagerly, without need or benefit of direction from someone in a higher position. See Exhibit 11.4 for a comparison of this style with the two previously discussed.

Open Management Style

In this model the organization functions very much as a biological organism. Each employee acts as a cell in the organism, knowing the functions and activities of all of the other employees, what information or services are required by other employees, and when the information or services are needed. There is

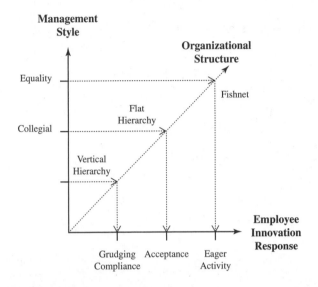

Exhibit 11.4   Third-Level Relationship and Organizational Linkages

no need for leaders at all. All of the information required for managing and running the organization is already embedded in each of the employees or organization members. There is no initiation by management, because there is no management. There is no employee response, because there is nothing to respond to. The organization operates efficiently and effectively without benefit of leadership. See Exhibit 11.5 for a comparison of all four management styles.

When interpersonal and structural relationship barriers to innovation and knowledge sharing are removed, innovation and creativity flourish naturally. As Exhibit 11.6 shows, the degree to which these barriers exist is the degree to which organizations need to initiate programs to artificially stimulate innovation and sharing. When relationship and structural solutions are not in place or are ineffective, incentive and reward systems are brought into play.

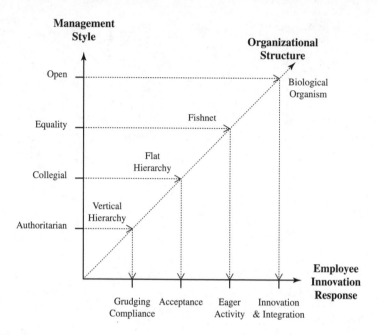

Exhibit 11.5   Fourth-Level Relationship and Organizational Linkages

Managerial Style	Authoritarian	Collegial	Egalitarian	Open
Organizational Structure	Vertical Hierarchy	Flat Hierarchy	Fishnet	Biological Organism
Innovation Response	Grudging Compliance	Acceptance	Eager Activity	Involvement & Integration
Need for Alignment	Low	High	High	High
Need for Incentives and Rewards	High	High	Low	Low

Exhibit 11.6   Summary of Relationship and Structural Trade-offs

THE USEFULNESS OF SOFTWARE TOOLS WITH CREATIVITY-FOCUSED HUMAN CAPITAL

At a recent demonstration by Aurigin System, Inc. (a company creating and selling software that allows firms to manage their intellectual property business assets), a representative had downloaded a portion of the patent portfolio of a Fortune 100 company from the U.S. Patent database to demonstrate Aurigin's system capabilities. In the demonstration Aurigin listed all of the demonstration company's patents within the pre-selected area of technology. Listed next to each patent was the name of the inventor. A second list showed the names of all of the inventors listed alphabetically and, next to each, all of that person's patents as well as the company employing them at the time the patent was filed. The list was startling.

For most of the inventors, the patents listed next to their name were filed by the company used for the demonstration, but a number of the inventors had moved from one company to another, as evidenced by the different company names next to one or more of their patents. Because of their demonstrated flexibility in employment, these inventors might more easily be persuaded to change companies than their fellow employees. The listing of inventors, patents, and companies could be used by a competitor to see which of the demonstration company's inventors might be most susceptible to being hired away!

To make the demonstration even more interesting, the Aurigin people said that when they installed their system in a client's organization, the installation team was told to identify the current use of each patent in the portfolio and, where possible, to link each patent to a product or service of the firm. Once again, the implications of this were startling! By linking the Aurigin software to the firm's financial information system, one could identify, for each inventor of the firm, the dollar amount of income the firm was realizing from each of the products and services resulting from the patents of a particular inventor.

Those few employees whose ideas and innovations are demonstrably providing identifiable amounts of income to the firm are more precious to the firm than are other employees and information technology now makes it possible to quantify, in dollar terms, the relative value of the firm's *core human capital*. Non-core employees, whose skills and abilities, while certainly valuable, are more easily replaceable than the core employees. Would not firms want to manage core human capital differently from non-core?

THE PRODUCTIVITY FOCUS FOR HUMAN CAPITAL

In companies that directly commercialize the knowledge of their human capital, the emphasis is on making that human capital more productive. These firms tend to bill for services by the hour. A client is billed based on the number of hours that employees of the direct services firm devote to the client's problems or issues. Direct services firms soon come to realize that there is a natural limit to the number of hours available for billing. For this reason, the emphasis for these firms is on making their human capital as productive as possible, minimizing the portion of their time devoted to non-billable activity and maximizing their productivity for clients.

Firms in this category seek out technology that improves the productivity of their human capital. It is common to see doctors, lawyers, consultants, et. al., frequently using laptop computers, portable telephones, pagers, electronic assistants, and wireless communication devices of all kinds. Every minute of the time of each element of the firm's human capital must be utilized to its fullest extent in order to best leverage its profitability. Maximizing value extraction, in the case of the human capital for discrete service firms, means maximizing the productivity of the human capital.

SUMMARY

The management of human capital, when viewed from a value extraction perspective, takes on a clarity of purpose not necessarily made obvious when looked at from the more traditional perspectives. The use of an intellectual capital framework makes it clear that firms have core human capital comprised of a small number of individuals whose creativity or productivity are crucial to the firm's ability to generate either current or future revenues and profits. Firms can identify the specific "core" employees and can take steps to ensure that they (and their knowledge) do not leave the firm; these steps may include obtaining some form of intellectual capital insurance.

There are two different areas of focus for the managers of human capital wishing to extract value. One focus, for firms who leverage their human capital through its codified knowledge, is to increase the level of creativity and new knowledge as well as the amount of valuable codified knowledge. The second is for firms that directly commercialize the knowledge of their human capital. These direct service firms are concerned with the productivity of their core human capital. For firms such as these, management focuses on minimizing the amount of time the core human capital must devote to non-billable activities. Technology plays an important role for the direct service firms because it may be used to increase the billable productivity of the core staff.

12

Making It Happen

Although worldwide there are only one hundred or so firms systematically extracting value from their intellectual capital, there are hundreds of firms that would like to do so. What stops companies in the second group from becoming like the first is knowing where and how to begin. Most companies that want to develop the capability for managing their intellectual capital have little or no understanding of what it takes. Members of the ICM Gathering all report that they receive dozens, perhaps hundreds, of calls each year from companies that want to learn how ICM is done. Because we are all eager to share what we have learned, we put aside time to meet with these companies. When the meetings began and we started talking about decision processes, work processes, data bases, and know-how, the visitors were overwhelmed by what they heard. Many had believed that the secret to intellectual capital management was a matter of learning one or two key concepts and acquiring some software that would do the job. They were overwhelmed to find out that installing an ICM capability involves philosophy, the company's vision and values, decision-making processes involving senior executives, and many more elements.

Managing intellectual capital, like many worthwhile business activities, is a commitment. It involves developing a capability that results from a logical and systematic set of activities, beginning with a crisp understanding of the firm's purpose and direction and the careful crafting of mechanisms to produce a desired set of results. This chapter discusses each step in the process and suggests how to take them successfully.

THE FOUNDATION

To begin, it is necessary for the firm to establish its IC framework. What is its vision for itself in the future? What kind of firm does it aspire to become? A journey without a destination may of course be interesting, enriching, and educational, but such a journey will be neither direct nor without frustration.

Many firms do not have a statement of vision; even those that do may not have developed a vision that adequately describes the business it wishes to become. Most firms I deal with in my consulting practice fall into this category. Getting around this lack of a formal vision is actually fairly simple. I usually bring together two or three knowledgeable senior employees and ask them to explain the real vision of the firm. Based on their knowledge of the company and its business trajectory, I ask them to describe the target the firm is aiming toward in the future. Most often these descriptions are anecdotal, and they are not necessarily complete. Nevertheless, each person's description of the firm's vision tends to complement that of the others. I usually take notes during these meetings, then summarize the employees' comments in the form of a bulleted list of descriptors of the company "in the future." We may modify the list, adding new statements and deleting others, but from this list, a working vision for the company is drafted.

With a company's formal vision statement or a working vision available, the next step is to know what the company's strategy is to achieve the vision. Many companies have a well-known and articulated strategy; others do not. For those without a formal strategy, a process similar to the working vision process is used to define the strategy of the firm. For purposes of the ICM capability-building project, a working strategy is an adequate substitute for a formal one. (For more information on how to create *useful* statements of vision and strategy, see the Appendix.)

The final step in creating the foundation is to determine the role(s) a company's intellectual capital could or should play in enabling its strategy and achieving its vision. Roles should be listed under the two headings we have already discussed: value creation and value extraction.

THE CONTEXT

Every company, like every individual, exists in a world of its own. Each company has unique aspirations, strengths, weaknesses, resources, values, external realities, internal dynamics, and personalities, as well as its own politics and worldview. No two companies operate in exactly the same context, even companies in the same or similar business or industry. Coca-Cola and Pepsi, both alike in many ways, have different contexts. They share many of the same external realities but differ in their internal realities. They have different visions and strategies, as well as different personalities among the top executives, complementary business assets, financial and organizational structures, and sets of intellectual capital. Their internal contexts are simply different. Because of their different contexts, an idea that is rejected at one of these firms as silly or unworkable may be seen by the other as creative, insightful, or valuable.

Creating a capability for managing the firm's intellectual capital is made easier by first understanding and articulating its context, for the context will determine what capabilities the firm will support. Context usually consists of three major elements: the business description, the external realities, and the internal realities. For each of these, few firms have an accurate (or politically acceptable) description of "what is." Most often, a firm has a party line that describes the view it wishes people to accept rather than a description of what is. The exercise of defining the firm's context is an exercise in defining "what is."

Business Description

Most firms have literature describing themselves, their products, services, and markets, but often firms do not adequately acknowledge the business they are really in. For example, some time ago I was doing a consulting assignment for the chairman of the Southland Corporation, the parent company of 7-Eleven convenience stores. At the time, 7-Eleven was the largest retailer of gasoline in the United States. In most states its convenience stores sold gasoline at retail, in addition to their familiar food and home convenience products. The chairman was faced with internal pressure to purchase a gasoline refinery on the Gulf Coast of the United States. Acquisition of the refinery, proponents argued, would integrate the company vertically and allow it to profit from refining as well as retailing gasoline. The analyses presented to the chairman made persuasive arguments about enhanced profits, ability to sell the by-products of gasoline refining to industrial customers, and so forth. I remember clearly a conversation in which the chairman said that his intuition was against the purchase, but he needed back-up data and analysis to buttress his intuition. I told him that he and his firm had made a multi-billion-dollar success out of the convenience store business, one they understood and in which they had significant experience, but once that refinery was purchased, they would be in the petroleum business, and all of their convenience store know-how would not help them at all.

Within two weeks the chairman called to say that all of the purchase papers were prepared for his signature and he needed my recommendations, even though he understood we had barely begun this complex financial analysis. I told him I could not yet give him any better answer than I already had—that purchasing the refinery would change the business Southland was really in. Southland would no longer be in the convenience store business. Despite my comments, and lacking any hard data to back up his intuition, he decided to bow to the internal analyses and purchase the refinery. Six months later he called to tell me I was right and just thought I would like to know. He went on to say that he now spent virtually all of his time tracking down tanker loads of crude oil to feed the refinery as well as industrial customers to purchase the non-gasoline output from the refinery, purchases that were necessary to make the refinery fully profitable. As a result, he felt that he might have been neglecting the convenience store aspect of the corporation's business. The purchase of the refinery proved to be the beginning of the end for the chairman and for Southland as it had been as a company. Eventually Southland went through a series of stock repurchases and restructurings, the chairman departed, and the refinery was sold. The company is now back in the convenience store business. The lesson: be sure you know the business you are really in, and be in that business.

The External Context

The forces in the firm's external environment that drive change in the economy, the industry, and the business make up the external context of the firm. Most firms can name the forces that most immediately affect their business, such as changes in the price of raw materials, the general state of the economy, and competing products or competitive thrusts. But few understand the forces that underlie these near-term forces for change. The external context of the firm includes the macro-economic, legislative, regulatory, technological, and socio-political forces that drive the firm's business environment. These need to be defined and described, and the nature of their impact on the firm needs to be known. Once these tasks are accomplished, these forces can be categorized as major and minor effects and as effects that are expected to be felt in the immediate, mid-, or long term. The key external forces for change and their leading indicators must be determined and monitored.

The Internal Context

The internal context is in many ways easier to determine because much of it is already known, if not yet fully articulated. The internal context usually includes:

- The firm's vision, strategy, and business goals
- The firm's values and culture
- An assessment of the firm's strengths and weaknesses to perform in the business it is really in
- Strategies available to the firm, not only those it is pursuing but also alternative strategies for achieving its vision
- Current performance against goals
- Potential usefulness of IC IA/IP in achieving the company's vision and strategy
- Current posture of the company on ICM (favorably disposed, strongly against, etc.)

Having defined the three major elements of context for the firm, it is particularly helpful to document what has been learned. Some firms have gone so far as to create an internal report that captures this information. Such a report might contain information such as:

- The strategic vision of the firm
- A definition of the business the firm is in
- Macro-environmental forces: overview of the macro-environment and key forces for change
- A definition of the firm's products and services and where each one is in its life cycle
- The basis for competition: cost or differentiation
- A description of the technology strategy
- Current firm performance, both measures and measurements

212

DEFINING THE ROLE OF
INTELLECTUAL CAPITAL

Once the firm's vision and strategy are understood, the role(s) for intellectual capital can be defined. For service firms, these roles tend to be offensive. The firm's IC is intimately involved with activities that directly affect revenue generation. For technology-based knowledge companies, on the other hand, the role of the technical human capital is fundamentally defensive: to create a set of patents that surround and defend the firm's key innovations and thereby prevent competitors from bringing the same (or perhaps similar) innovations into the market. Once the patents have been developed, these firms use them defensively, fending off copycats. For these companies the defensive posture involves the creation of legal protection that allows subsequent exclusive exploitation of innovations. In addition to assuring exclusive use, defensive use of the firm's intellectual assets includes avoiding litigation and developing some freedom to use a technology in the future.

Increasingly, however, many firms like those described above are using their intellectual capital offensively as well. It may be used to generate new streams of revenue. Firms may use the portfolio to generate income they otherwise might have forgone. They may license core or strategic technologies into new markets that do not compete with their strategic or core markets. They may license or sell no-longer strategic technologies into existing markets. They may license both core and non-core technologies into non-strategic markets. Companies may also create de facto technology standards by cross-licensing with business or technology competitors to create a market for new or downstream technologies yet to be developed. They may simply license out company technology because its widespread use will create a de facto standard, thereby forcing competitors to seek a license in order to produce products or services consistent with the newly established standard. Finally, many companies have learned that they cannot afford to maintain the range of competencies and skills required to sustain their product line. Those companies may create strategic alliances with firms that have the capabilities they need. Successful negotiations with such alliance partners are often enabled by the presence of strong portfolios of intellectual assets and intellectual properties.

Still another role for intellectual capital may lie in its use to support the strategic position of the firm. Making the outside world aware of the firm's capabilities, its stocks of IC, and its ability to leverage them may position the firm in a marketplace or it may provide access to financial capital that otherwise might not be available on favorable terms or not at all.

Whether the role of intellectual capital is determined to be tactical or strategic, immediate or long term, or internally or externally oriented, it should be clear that there are many more roles for intellectual capital in firms that have carefully set a goal for the future. Such decisions make it easier to determine how intellectual capital, as well as other strategic assets of the firm, may be used to achieve the desired results.

DESIGNING THE SYSTEM

Once the role of intellectual capital in the firm is determined, the managers of the firm's intellectual capital need to develop the internal capabilities for exploiting it in meaningful ways. Beginning with the technology-based knowledge company, this section describes where and how to begin the process of creating the capability for managing intellectual capital.

Begin with the IP Portfolio

This section pertains to companies with at least one portfolio of intellectual properties. For such companies the place to begin is with the best-defined portfolio. Typically this is the patent portfolio.

Define the Portfolio

Managing intellectual properties means first identifying the properties to be managed. Patents or the rights to patents constitute the company's portfolio. The first question to be asked is, What does the portfolio contain? Are the patents known? (Surprisingly, many companies cannot identify the patents they own.)

Design the IPM System

Describe the IP management system the firm ultimately wishes to create. Include the basic functional elements as well as the decision processes, their supporting work processes, and databases. (In Chapter 2, the section entitled "The Third Dimension: IC Activities" there is a description of the generic IPM system.) The system design at this stage should be at the overview level. (Detailed design information is not necessary at this early stage, and could even be a non-productive diversion.) The overview IPM system design developed here becomes the template the firm works toward implementing.

Define the Portfolio Database

In addition to hard copies of each patent, effective patent management demands that there be a computer file containing useful information about each patent. This information will be needed to make informed decisions about portfolio management, business tactics, and business strategy.

Establish the Competitive Assessment Activity

Fundamental to managing the firm's intellectual property is an understanding of the competition. The firm needs to know, for both its business and its technology competitors, what they have produced, what their current position and capabilities are, what their strategies are, and what actions can be expected from them in the future. Competitive assessment should be performed by people with business as well as technical analytical backgrounds. Many technology firms try to convert technologists into business analysts on the mistaken assumption that business analysis is relatively easy if one has a scientific or analysis background. But business analysis requires the kind of special training found in university-level business or economics programs. Anything less than this level of training is not recommended.

Create a Patent Policy for the Firm

In an ideal world, businesses would only develop innovations that are in line with their strategy or that enable their vision. The real world is, unfortunately, less than ideal. Innovators produce what they produce, and these innovations are not all consistent with the vision or the strategy. To make decision-making easier, firms have found it useful to establish patenting guidelines or policy. Patent policies span the range of possibilities:

- Patent in order to have a portfolio with which to negotiate business agreements (licenses, joint ventures, alliances, et al.) with other companies.
- Upon brief examination, patent most things that have a chance of achieving technical success.
- After careful scrutiny, patent only those discoveries that have a strong chance of achieving technical success regardless of potential business application or use.
- Patent only those discoveries that have a clear application to your own company's products or processes.
- Patent discoveries that might block or delay similar discoveries by competitors.
- Patent most things that are patentable.
- Patent only the occasional discovery of exceptional importance.
- Do not patent anything.

Regularize the Patent Generation Process

All technology firms have a process of some kind that produces innovations targeted for patenting. Not all of the innovations produced are of patentable quality; and even if they were, the firm might not wish to invest in patenting them. While the patenting policy provides one level of decision-making guidance, many more innovations clear the policy guideline hurdle than the firm may wish to patent. The decision to patent is best made in the context of the firm's business strategy, the dollar amount in the budget it has reserved to cover the costs of patenting, and the set of patentable innovations available for consideration.

Firms that want to ensure an adequate flow of innovations into that patent decision process create information processes that highlight innovations under development. This allows them to determine whether sufficient numbers of innovations are in process to meet their strategic needs, whether too many are in process in one technology area and not enough in another, or whether not enough innovations are in process at all. The firm's existing system for monitoring what is in the pipeline and for making the patent decision should be regularized and perhaps made more efficient. Such a regularization will allow the firm to know that it has a sufficient number and quality of innovations to meet its needs.

Develop a Valuation Process

Create an organizational capability for developing both qualitative and dollar-based estimates of the value of the firm's intellectual assets. The capability should include valuation methods that provide dollar values ranging from coarse valuation to fine.

Develop a Value-Extraction Analysis Capability

For each technology with the potential for commercialization, several questions must be answered before the company can decide to invest in commercialization, including: Which combination of conversion mechanisms should the firm use to extract the most value from the innovation? Should the firm: sell the innovation, license it, create a joint venture to obtain necessary complementary assets, enter into a strategic alliance to obtain access to markets, integrate everything, or donate the technology for a tax benefit? Each technology requires an analysis to determine how many of the conversion mechanisms the firm can use to obtain the best profit results from the innovation.

Create a Licensing/Joint Venture/Alliance Capability

Once the firm has decided to commercialize an innovation, it needs the capability to make the commercialization happen. In many cases this means commercializing the innovation through licensing, joint venturing, or entering into a strategic alliance. Firms must develop an office or a capability that will be able to expeditiously develop licensing, joint venture, and strategic alliance agreements and execute them for the firm.

Move on to Managing Intellectual Assets

At this point, firms that have created the foregoing capabilities have largely developed a systematic approach to managing their intellectual property. The next steps are described below.

Develop Portfolios of Non-Protected Assets

Create defined portfolios (and databases) for intellectual assets with commercial use or interest. The list of portfolios of non-protected assets might include licenses (both in- and out-licenses), non-disclosure agreements, joint venture agreements, outsourcing contracts and service agreements, IA aspects of mergers and acquisitions, and customer lists.

Develop IT Linkages Between Portfolios

Identify linkages between the IA portfolio databases. These might include company names, individuals' names, technologies, products, or services.

Expand Competitive Assessment

Whereas the IP-level of competitive assessment has already been developed, assessing IAs may involve gathering information about the specific marketplace positions and long-term strategies of competitors for use in strategic arrangements and outsourcing, and determining the specific value of the current and potential portfolio based on its effect on competitors (e.g., infringements and design-arounds, as well as predicted competitor response to potential strategic thrusts).

Create Litigation Avoidance Analytical Capability

The ability to know when and how a company is at risk of infringement litigation is important. Perhaps of even greater importance is whether potential litigants are infringing upon the firm's intellectual property and whether the competitor has previously signed a non-disclosure agreement or is party to a contract or supplier agreement. All of this information, when correlated, is part of the creation of a viable litigation avoidance capability.

Managing Intellectual Capital

Firms that manage their intellectual capital are strategically focused on managing both the human and the paper assets of the firm. For these firms the emphasis is on strategy and strategic positioning—how to use the firm's intellectual capital. For the subset of these firms that includes technology companies, the building block capabilities are already in place, but non-technology (the alternate subset) companies need to ensure that all of the following capabilities are in place before proceeding.

Competitive Assessment

The competitive assessment focuses on the business and technology competitors: the technology of competitive products, services, and markets, as well as the competitors' human capital.

Management of Human Capital

In the management of the firm's human capital it is important to understand the firm's current and ideal use of its human resources. What is the ideal allocation of the firm's human capital for achieving near-term goals? Long-term goals? What is its actual current alignment? What is the value-creation focus of the human capital? What know-how has the human capital created? How is this know-how defined? How is it described? What is the firm's ability to access it? What is the firm's ability to commercialize it? How can the firm develop or improve systems to institutionalize the management of its human capital?

Measurement of Human Capital

How does the firm define, describe, and measure its intellectual capital? What kinds of knowledge does the firm's HC generate? How wide and how deep is the knowledge created by the human capital?

Reporting on Intellectual Capital

What kinds of reports does the firm have or wish to have about its intellectual capital? Internal reports? External reports? Do these include measures of key IC activities? Do they include valuations of the firm's human capital?

COMMUNICATING THE VALUE OF IC TO THE FIRM

Obtaining consensus on the value of IC to the firm is an important step in the process of creating the capability. Where there is acceptance and interest in installing an IC capability, it is easier to obtain the top management support and the resources required to proceed. Communications should proceed upward to the executive suite in order to obtain backing and resources and outward throughout the organization to gain awareness, interest, and general support. Communicating upward involves meeting with senior executives to make them aware, to garner backing, to obtain spending approval, and to generate continuing interest and backing. Communicating outward may be done through multiple channels, including traditional ones such as newsletters, group meetings, and speeches, and new ones such as a company intranet or e-mail. Outward communication might extend beyond the firm's employees to some of the firm's stakeholders: vendors, suppliers, shareholders, customers, and others. For each communication channel, the message communicated should be tailored for the audience in terms of length, breadth, frequency, and style.

Every firm I have talked with about intellectual capital and ICM, including every member of the ICM Gathering, has found it difficult to communicate the value of intellectual capital within the firm. Using the experiences of more than two dozen companies, I have developed an approach to communicating the value of intellectual capital. The following are the elements of an internal communication program.

Create the IC Story

The IC story is the firm's IC message. The story should contain information that will convince the audience, even one comprised of skeptics, of the importance of IC to their own firm. It should define intellectual capital and explain why and how other companies have found it to be important, how it is (or could be) of value to your firm, and how the capability is (or could be) created at your firm. The IC story should be created with both internal and external audiences in mind. For the internal audience, the IC story should convey information about the importance of IC, the kind of value the firm seeks to obtain from its IC, the firm's context for its IC, the way in which the firm is organized to take advantage of its IC, and the firm-wide measures of IC that describe to insiders what the firm's IC is, where it is located, and how the firm is leveraging it for value.

The external audience for the firm's IC story is often comprised of stakeholders and interested observers (financial analysts, government regulators, et. al.). The external IC story should contain all of the elements of the internal story plus several others. It should also explain how the firm's IC and its management create corporate value that outsiders will find of value to them. For example, the external story might discuss how the firm's IC contributes to its valuation and thereby to its stock price. The story might explain the effect the firm's IC has on its vendors, suppliers, and customers. The IC story, in short, should contain the following elements:

The Role of IC in Company Strategy

Set forth the company's strategy and the potential role IC could play in that strategy. Is the company IC rich? Does it have unextracted value from its current stock of intellectual properties, intellectual assets, or intellectual capital? What role does IC currently play in the company's strategy? What roles could it play?

Examples of Success and Failure

Provide examples of the *successes* some companies have had in managing their intellectual capital: in terms of income generation (Texas Instruments, IBM), stock price increase (Skandia), finding hidden value (Dow), creating a powerful portfolio (Hewlett-Packard, Xerox), and creating new value (Swirl, Intel). Also provide examples of companies that failed to grasp the basic concepts of ICM such as: Xerox and the personal computer, Apple and software out-licensing, and EMI and the loss of its CAT-scan business.

The Hook

Using the company context as the basis, find the argument that compels the listener to agree that managing the firm's intellectual capital will be valuable to the company and that, indeed, the company should be leveraging its intellectual capital as part of its strategy and vision-achieving activities.

Outline the Capability-Building Process

It is not enough to convince someone of the value IC could bring to the firm; one must at the same time demonstrate what it would take for the company to realize that value. It is important to develop a clear project plan for creating the capability. The plan should describe what capability is desired, outline the major steps (and milestones), and provide a road map and time-table. A detailed plan and schedule are an important follow-up to the IC story.

SUMMARY

This chapter has identified the steps required of companies that want to implement an ICM capability. While the chapter is focused on the issues facing technology companies, much of what is included relates to all knowledge companies, not just those commercializing technology. The areas of greatest importance are defining the firm's vision and long-term strategy, describing the context within which the firm operates, defining the role(s) for intellectual capital, designing the IP and IA management systems, and describing and implementing the IC management capability desired by the firm. The steps outlined in this chapter are gleaned from the experiences of all of the firms in the ICM Gathering.

The importance of the building blocks cannot be stated too strongly. Firms without a clearly articulated vision and strategy will have difficulty implementing an effective ICM capability. Where a vision and a long-term strategy do not formally exist, create de facto working outlines for them. It is also vitally important to make explicit the firm's context and its internal and external realities. Without a thorough understanding of the context it is impossible to create and utilize intellectual capital within the firm to its best advantage. With these two basic building blocks in place it is possible to design, implement, and operate effective systems for managing and utilizing the firm's intellectual capital. Without them, the likelihood of success diminishes.

APPENDIX

Basic Definitions and Concepts

This appendix is included to reinforce the reader's knowledge of the basic concepts that underlie this book. It provides a brief overview of the evolution of intellectual capital management (ICM) as a working discipline. This evolution involves not only the concepts upon which intellectual capital management is based, but also the evolution of the thinking about those concepts.

This appendix is divided into the following three sections: Basic Concepts and Definitions for IC and ICM, A Brief History of the ICM Movement, and Management Concepts.

BASIC CONCEPTS AND DEFINITIONS FOR IC AND ICM

A Need for Common Definitions

Discussions about intellectual capital can be confusing because of a lack of common definitions for frequently used terms. The reasons for this are twofold. First, managers of intellectual capital use different models or perspectives, each of which describes intellectual capital differently. For example, there are both knowledge-based and economic-based views of intellectual capital (IC). Depending on which view or model is used, the commonly used terms have different meanings. This appendix defines the perspective or the intellectual capital model, the terms, and the definitions that are used throughout this book.

Second, each organization has its own world view. Within that world view each organization is faced with a different set of external and internal realities. The world view combined with the internal and external realities form the context within which each firm defines, manages, and values its intellectual capital. When two firms with different contexts discuss how best to manage intellectual capital, they will find communication and agreement difficult. This appendix discusses some of the principal elements of context and how they affect a firm's management of its intellectual capital.

Intellectual Capital Management

Since its origins in the 1980s, the motivation, as well as the new ideas and innovations in the field, have been developed almost entirely by the companies actively managing their IC. Through the experiences of these companies the field of ICM has evolved into two distinct areas of focus: *value creation* and *value extraction.*

Value creation concerns the generation of new knowledge *and* its conversion into innovations with commercial value. In the area of value creation, the management focus is on people, the human capital. Value creation activities include training, education, knowledge, innovation, building organizational structures, developing organizational and individual customer relationships, and managing values and culture.

Value extraction involves converting the created value into a form that is useful to the organization. This often involves converting a firm's innovations into cash or into some form of strategic position. Typically, value creation involves using the codified knowledge created by an organization's human capital to create valuations, decision processes, databases, screening and culling, conversion mechanisms, and asset management systems and capabilities.

Intellectual Capital

The new term used to describe a company that focuses on intellectual capital is a *knowledge company*. Knowledge companies use their knowledge (intellectual capital) as a major source of competitive advantage. They use their specific product or market knowledge to differentiate themselves from their competitors. Indeed, knowledge companies are leveraging newly defined kinds of capital: human, structural, and intellectual.

This discussion will focus primarily on intellectual capital because it is viewed by knowledge companies as their source of competitive advantage. What exactly is intellectual capital?

Although there are many descriptions of what constitutes intellectual capital (see Exhibit A.1), virtually everyone agrees that intellectual capital includes a range of knowledge, lore, ideas, and innovations. We also know that industrial knowledge may be divided into two kinds, tacit and codified, as defined in Exhibit A.2. Codified knowledge is knowledge that

• Inventions	• Data
• Technologies	• Skills
• Ideas	• Processes
• General Knowledge	• Creativity
• Computer Programs	• Publications
• Designs	• Drawings

Exhibit A.1   What Constitutes Intellectual Capital

Source: Patrick H. Sullivan, *Profiting from Intellectual Capital: Extracting Value from Innovation.* Copyright © 1998 by John Wiley & Sons, Inc. Reprinted by permission of John Wiley & Sons, Inc.

Industrial Knowledge		
	Tacit	Codified
Definition	Knowledge which is difficult to articulate and may be embedded in ways of doing things	Knowledge which is written down in some medium.
Ownership	Ownership resides with the holder of the know-how; difficult to copy and/or transfer	Technology easier to protect using the mechanism of the law; yet also easier to transfer
Examples	Experience Lore Group Skills	Blueprints Code Formulae Computer Programs

Exhibit A.2   Types of Industrial Knowledge

Source: Patrick H. Sullivan, *Profiting from Intellectual Capital: Extracting Value from Innovation.* Copyright © 1998 by John Wiley & Sons, Inc. Reprinted by permission of John Wiley & Sons, Inc.

has been committed to some form of communication medium. It might be a handwritten document, a computer program, a blueprint, or a cartoon.

Tacit knowledge resides within an individual, often as a skill, an ability, or know-how. It can be demonstrated or taught to others. Examples of tacit knowledge and abilities are artistic skills such as pottery, sculpture, and painting. Although in modern times these skills have become codified, in earlier days such knowledge was passed from teacher to student, and from master to apprentice.

In knowledge companies, intellectual capital comprises both tacit and codified knowledge. From the perspective of someone wanting to extract value from it, a working definition of intellectual capital is knowledge that can be converted into profit. Exhibit A.3 shows that there are two major components of intellectual capital: human capital and intellectual assets.

Intellectual Capital

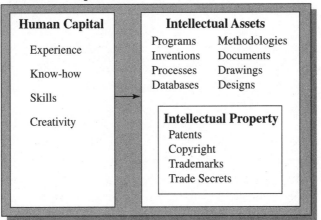

Exhibit A.3   The Intellectual Capital of the Firm

The distinction between human capital and intellectual assets is of particular importance to owners of knowledge companies. Unlike human capital (people), which is not interchangeable and cannot be owned by shareholders, intellectual assets are and can be. For this reason, it is clearly to the advantage of the knowledge firm to transform the innovations produced by its human capital into intellectual assets to which the firm can assert rights of ownership. One major task of IC managers is to transform human (tacit) capital into intellectual (codified) assets.

Human Capital

The human capital of the firm may be defined as the capabilities of employees, contractors, suppliers, and other company-related people to solve customer problems. The firm-wide human capital resource is the know-how and institutional memory about topics of importance to the company. The human capital includes the collective experience, skills, and general know-how of all of the firm's people. It is a resource because it can generate value for the company, yet it would be difficult for the company to deliver this value without the employees themselves. For example, a law firm might count its staff of lawyers as its income-producing or commercializable human capital. The lawyers appear in court and advise clients on legal matters. It is difficult to imagine how a law firm could provide such legal services to its clients without the carrier of the skills, the lawyer.

Other kinds of companies use their human capital very differently in creating value. A software company may use its programmers to create a new software program. The program, once codified, becomes an intellectual asset that can be reproduced, manufactured, and sold to customers. In this case, the human capital does not create value for the customer directly, as the lawyer does, but indirectly, by creating an intellectual asset that can be manufactured and sold.

Codifying knowledge is not easy. It requires managers to convince the firm's human capital that they can and should commit their ideas to the firm in writing. But it is often difficult to know which employees have valuable knowledge and whether that knowledge can be accessed. When companies are small it is easy for everyone to know what information is relevant to a situation and how to gain access to the knowledge possessed by individuals within the firm. As companies grow and become more complex, and the size of the human capital pool increases, such information is less widely shared and becomes more compartmentalized. In an ideal world the corporation could evolve to possess some form of collective intelligence (a term coined by George Por, founder of Community Intelligence Labs), in which all members of the organization have access to all of the firm's relevant knowledge, instantly available at all times. With increasing size it becomes even more important for knowledge firms to motivate their human capital resources to codify their knowledge and know-how, in order to more widely share it and inculcate it into the firm.

Intellectual Assets

Intellectual assets, the second component of IC, are the codified, tangible, or physical descriptions of specific knowledge to which the company can assert ownership rights. Any piece of knowledge that becomes defined, usually by being written down or input into a computer, qualifies as an intellectual asset and can be protected. Intellectual assets are the source of innovations that the firm commercializes.

Intellectual assets that receive legal protection are *intellectual property*. Intellectual property law, which deals with the protection of intellectual assets, recognizes five forms of legal protection in the United States: patents, copyrights, trade secrets, trademarks, and semiconductor masks. For each protected intellectual asset, the nature and amount of protection available varies, as does the degree to which that protection applies to an idea or innovation.

Intellectual assets, by definition, may be legally protected. Indeed, regardless of whether formal legal protection is sought, intellectual assets are usually protected by the trade secret provisions of the law. A firm may choose not to legally protect all of its intellectual assets. Nevertheless, both intellectual assets and intellectual properties are the most usual elements of intellectual capital to be commercialized.

Structural Capital

Intellectual capital by itself is of little value without the leveraging effect of the firm's supporting resources, called *structural capital*. Structural capital is the support or infrastructure that firms provide to their human capital. It includes both direct and indirect support, and for each there are both physical and intangible elements. Direct support, which touches the human capital directly, includes physical elements such as computers, desks, and telephones, and intangible elements such as information systems, computer software, work procedures, marketing plans, and company know-how. Indirect support, which does not touch the human capital directly, includes such physical elements as buildings, lights, electricity, and plumbing, and intangible elements such as strategic plans, payroll systems, cost structures, and supplier relationships. Indeed, structural capital provides the environment that encourages the human capital to create and leverage its knowledge. The structural capital is the part of the firm that remains in place when the human capital goes home.

Complementary business assets are one element of the firm's structural capital that deserves special mention. These are the business assets of the firm that are used to create value in the commercialization process. Typically, for knowledge companies, the business assets of the firm complement the innovations developed by the human capital. These complementary business assets typically include manufacturing facilities, distribution networks, customer lists and relationships, supplier networks, service forces, complementary technologies, trademarks, and organization capabilities. Complementary assets may be thought of as the string of assets through which the innovations must be processed in order to reach the customer. No matter how exciting an intellectual asset itself may be, it will have little commercial value unless paired with the appropriate complementary assets.

There are two kinds of complementary assets. The first are business assets that are widely available—*generic business assets*. They can be bought or contracted for on the open market and may be used in commercializing a wide range of technology applications. The second kind, which offer more leverage, differentiate the firm from others in its industry. Economists call these *unique complementary assets* because they are unique to the firm *and* they complement the innovations of its human capital. Suppose an inventor devised a unique product with a large market appeal. If this product could be made using manufacturing equipment that is readily available in the marketplace, then its manufacture would involve the use of generic assets. If, on the other hand, the product required some manufacturing process or technique that was unique to the technology or the example firm's product design (so that generic manufacturing equipment was not capable of producing it), then that specific manufacturing capability of the firm would be a *unique* or *firm-specific complementary asset.* A specific complementary business asset can be used strategically as a barrier to competition; licensed out as a source of income; sold; or used to attract joint venture partners. Most important, it can be used to protect a technology from competitors when legal protection is either not desired or not available.

Specific complementary assets, then, are a source of value in addition to the value created by the innovation. The use of a business asset in the commercialization process adds value to the innovation on its way to the marketplace. It is this additional value that the owner of the complementary asset can capture and retain. The value realized by the manufacturing process can be captured as profit by the owner of the manufacturing system, the value of distribution can be captured as profit by the owner of the distribution system, and so on. Where the business assets are unique to the innovation, their owners can charge a greater premium for the value they add to the innovation. Thus complementary business assets are also a source of hidden value; in fact, they provide a greater value to the firm than their mere tangible asset book value.

Specific complementary business assets are usually created in conjunction with the commercialization of a specific application of an intellectual asset. They are therefore unique, and often are themselves protectable by patents. In effect, controlling the specific complementary assets of the firm is equivalent to controlling the underlying intellectual asset and the ultimate commercial value of an intellectual asset. Obtaining patent protection for a unique complementary business asset has the advantage of protecting a technology without having to reveal the technology itself. Patenting the technology itself does not provide this advantage.

Value: Sources and Conversions

For a knowledge company, whose profits come primarily from the commercialization of its ideas and innovations, there are only two fundamental sources of value: the innovations themselves and the complementary business assets of the firm that are applied to the commercialization of its innovations. Further, there are only seven ways that firms can convert their product or service innovations into cash: direct sale, out-licensing, joint venture to obtain and use needed complementary business assets, strategic alliance to obtain and exploit markets, integration with current business, create a new business, and donation (tax write-off). (See Exhibit A.4.)

For sophisticated knowledge companies, the route to maximizing profit extraction for any product or service innovation is to maximize the number of combinations of unique complementary business assets and conversion mechanisms. This means that for any one innovation, a firm would seek to license it in one market, establish a joint venture with another firm in a second market (and through the joint venture obtain cash), form

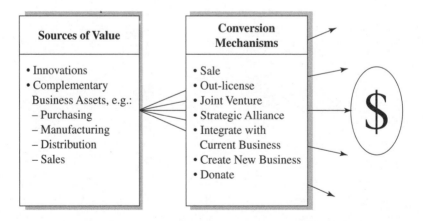

Exhibit A.4   Sources of Value and Conversion Mechanisms

Source: Patrick H. Sullivan, *Profiting from Intellectual Capital: Extracting Value from Innovation.* Copyright © 1998 by John Wiley & Sons, Inc. Reprinted by permission of John Wiley & Sons, Inc.

a strategic alliance with another firm in a third market, and integrate the entire operation in a fourth market.

The Commercialization Decision

Any firm that intends to commercialize an innovation should undertake an analysis of its profit extraction potential. The decision to commercialize should be made only after a firm answers a series of questions designed to determine the mechanism to be used to convert the technology to cash as well as the degree of risk involved in successfully completing the cash conversion (see Exhibit A.5).

When deciding how to extract the most value from an idea, the first question is, does the innovation meet a market need? If the answer is no, then the innovation has no immediate commercial value and should be stored until some other innovation is created which, when matched with the first, will produce something that does meet a market need. If the innovation meets a market need, then a second question can be asked.

The second question concerns whether legal protection is a competitive issue. For some innovations as well as for some industries, legal protection is not required in order for an innovation to be commercializable. Perhaps the most famous example is Coca-Cola. The formula for Coke syrup is a tightly held secret within the firm. To patent it legally, the firm would have to reveal the formula. Rather than do so, the firm maintains the formula as one of the best-kept secrets in the world. In most industries, however, legal protection for an innovation is necessary before the innovating firm will decide to invest its funds in commercialization. If protection is an issue, the related question involves the degree to which adequate protection is available. The adequacy of protection depends upon many things, usually a mixture of legal, technology, and business considerations. When the degree of protection is not considered adequate, the innovation is stored, awaiting an adequately protected partner innovation.

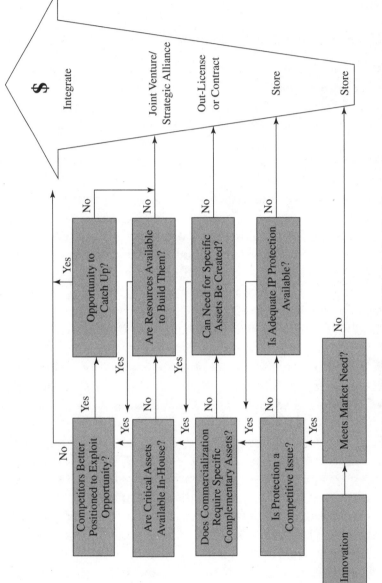

Exhibit A.5   The Commercialization Decision Process

Source: Patrick H. Sullivan, *Profiting from Intellectual Capital: Extracting Value from Innovation.* Copyright © 1998 by John Wiley & Sons, Inc. Reprinted by permission of John Wiley & Sons, Inc.

The third question concerns whether the innovation's commercialization requires specific complementary assets. In cases where commercialization does not require specific complementary assets, it must be determined whether the innovation could be redesigned or reconfigured to require specific complementary assets. The reason for this is simple. When specific complementary assets are required, the firm has the opportunity to obtain profits not only from the innovation, but from the unique complementary asset as well. Indeed, an innovation that requires more than one unique complementary asset has more value to the firm that owns those specific assets.

If the innovation under review does not require specific complementary assets for its commercialization, then the firm has a limited number of ways of profiting from the innovation. For this reason, it is often best to out-license the innovation to some firm that owns the generic assets required for commercialization. On completion of the out-licensing transaction, the firm should sequester the licensing income, look inside the firm for another innovation that requires specific complementary assets, and invest the licensing income in bringing that innovation to market.

If specific complementary assets are required, the next question is whether these assets are available in-house. If they are not, does the firm have the resources available to build, buy, or acquire these resources? If specific assets are required and the commercializing firm cannot obtain access to them directly, then the most profitable course of action is to find a firm that owns such assets and obtain access to them through a joint venture.

In the parlance of intellectual capital, a firm may consider three types of business alliance: a contract, used to obtain access to generic business assets; a joint venture, used to obtain access to specific business assets; or a strategic alliance, used to obtain access to markets.

If access to specific assets can be arranged, the final question is whether the commercializing firm is adequately positioned in the marketplace. The market competitive position of the firm is considered adequate if it has access to the market for the product. If other firms have better access, can the commercializing firm catch up? If the answer to these questions is no, then the commercializing firm should form a strategic alliance with the firm that does have access to the markets.

If, however, the commercializing firm has adequate access to the markets, then it should integrate the innovation, the protection, and the complementary assets and manufacture and bring the innovation to market itself. The further the firm can progress in the commercialization decision before settling on a conversion mechanism, the greater are the profits available. (It is also true, of course, that the greater the profit potential, the greater the risk.)

In summary, the commercialization decision involves asking five questions in sequence, the answers to which determine the optimum cash conversion mechanism for an innovation. The decision process relies upon a knowledge of several underlying concepts: complementary business assets, conversion mechanisms, and the sources of value from innovation.

A BRIEF HISTORY OF THE ICM MOVEMENT

The Conceptual Thinkers

The evolution of intellectual capital management as a discipline followed a pattern that is detectable in hindsight, although to the people involved at the beginning there was no pattern discernible at the time. There were three distinctly different origins of what has become the intellectual capital management movement. The first was in Japan with the groundbreaking work of Hiroyuki Itami, who studied the effect of *invisible assets* on the management of Japanese corporations. The second was the work of a disparate set of economists seeking a different view or theory of the firm. The views of these economists (Penrose, Rumelt, Wernerfelt, and others) were coalesced by David Teece of UC Berkeley in a seminal 1986 article on technology commercialization. Finally, the work of Karl-Eric Sveiby in Sweden, published originally in Swedish, addressed the human capital dimension of intellectual capital and, in so doing, provided a rich and tantalizing view of the potential for valuing the enterprise based upon the competences and knowledge of its employees.

Over the period 1959–1997 a diverse set of academic researchers and economists developed a new view on business strategy that emphasized resource efficiency rather than the generally accepted competitive forces. The resource-based perspective notes that firms have differentiated or unique resources, capabilities, and endowments. Further, these resource endowments are "sticky" (they are not easily added nor are they easily discarded), at least in the short run, so that firms must operate with what they have. The resources-based perspective focuses on strategies for exploiting existing firm-specific assets. Since some of the firm's assets are intellectual, it follows that issues such as skills acquisition, the management of knowledge and know-how, and learning become fundamental strategic issues. In this context, the work of Itami and Sveiby, dealing with invisible assets or human capital, may have enormous potential for contributing to business strategy.

There has been an increasing frequency and specificity of contribution to the field since its inception. The timeline in Exhibit A.6 shows the diversity of contributors and their influence on each other. The contributions of those whose names appear in the timelines in Exhibits A.6 and A.7 are briefly explained below.

Hiroyuki Itami—Itami's groundbreaking work on the value of invisible assets to the corporation was originally published in Japanese in 1980. Not published in English until 1987, it was slow to be found by people interested in intellectual assets, and therefore slow to be seen as a significant

1980	Itami publishes "Mobilizing Invisible Assets" in Japanese
1981	Hall establishes company to commercialize research on human values
1986	Sveiby publishes "The Know-How Company" on managing intangible assets
April 1986	Teece publishes seminal paper on extracting value from innovation
1988	Sveiby publishes "The New Annual Report" introducing "knowledge capital"
1989	Sveiby publishes "The Invisible Balance Sheet"
Summer 1989	Sullivan begins research into "commercializing innovation"
Fall 1990	Sveiby publishes "Knowledge Management"
Fall 1990	Term "Intellectual Capital" coined in Stewart's presence
Jan. 1991	Stewart publishes first "Brainpower" article in Fortune
Sept. 1991	Skandia organizes first corporate IC function, names Edvinsson VP
Spring 1992	Stewart publishes "Brainpower" article in *Fortune*
1993	St. Onge establishes concept of Customer Capital
July 1994	First meeting of Mill Valley Group
Oct. 1994	Stewart authors "Intellectual Capital" cover article in *Fortune*
Nov. 1994	Sullivan, Petrash, Edvinsson decide to host a gathering of IC managers
Jan. 1995	Second meeting Mill Valley Group
May 1995	First Skandia public report on IC
April 1996	SEC symposium on measuring intellectual/intangible assets
Sept. 1996	Sullivan and Parr book, *Licensing Strategies,* published
Oct. 1996	Lev founds Intangibles Research Project at New York University
Mar. 1997	Sveiby publishes "The New Organizational Wealth"
Mar. 1997	Edvinsson and Malone book, *Intellectual Capital,* published
April 1997	Stewart book, *Intellectual Capital,* published
June 1997	Hoover Institution conference on measuring intellectual capital
March 1998	Sullivan book, *Profiting from Intellectual Capital*, published

Exhibit A.6   Timeline of IC-Related Events

contribution to the field. Nevertheless, readers of Itami's work uniformly comment on its prescience and the clarity of its insights into intangible assets and their importance to the corporation.

David Teece—Teece's 1986 article "Profiting from Techno-logical Innovation" brought together much of the work done

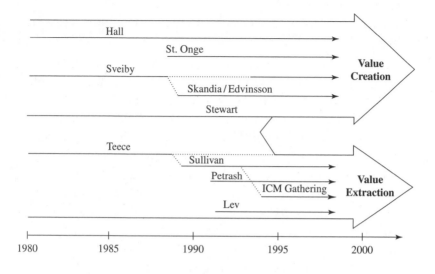

Exhibit A.7   Timeline and Relationships among ICM Contributors

by academic researchers and economists leading toward a resource-based theory of strategy. This article was instrumental in demonstrating the economist's view of technology commercialization and contained several ideas that were key to a management capability for extracting value from innovation. This article (and subsequent work) identified sources of value in technological innovation, the mechanisms for converting value to profits, and the steps necessary for commercializing innovation.

Brian Hall—For more than 25 years Hall has studied human values. In collaboration with Benjamin Tonna, he developed a hierarchy of human values as well as several instruments for measuring and describing the value sets of individuals and corporations. Hall founded Omega Associates in 1981 to commercialize his research. This company transitioned into Values Technology in 1989. Values Technology works with firms to identify their values, analyze how those values aid or impede firms' achievement of their business goals, and change the values, if necessary, to make them more supportive of the firms' business goals.

Karl-Erik Sveiby—Sveiby, currently Professor at Macquarie Graduate School of Management in Sydney, is the founding father of the very early "Swedish Movement" in knowledge management and intellectual capital. In 1986, he published his first book (written in Swedish) in which he explored how to manage the rapidly growing field of knowledge companies—organizations that have no traditional production, only the knowledge and creativity of their employees. In 1990, he published *Kunskapsledning* (written in Swedish), the world's first book dealing with knowledge management. Sveiby was the first to recognize the need to measure human capital, and he pioneered accounting practices for these intangible assets, testing them in his own company. In 1989, he published the results of a working group in the book *The Invisible Balance Sheet,* proposing a theory for measuring knowledge capital "by dividing it into three categories: *customer capital, individual capital,* and *structural capital.*" The approach was adopted by a large number of Swedish-listed companies and, in 1993, the Swedish Council of Service Industries adopted it as their standard recommendation for annual reports, the first ever standard in this field. One of the many people inspired by Sveiby's concepts was Leif Edvinsson. Edvinsson went on to relabel these intangible assets as *intellectual capital* when he produced Skandia's first annual report supplement on intellectual capital in 1995.

Hubert St. Onge—The father of the concept of customer capital, Hubert St. Onge is considered to be one of the most creative thinkers in the field of learning and knowledge management. St. Onge, responsible for developing learning programs for the Canadian International Bank of Commerce, was interested in how to translate learning into both human and structural capital. He began by exploring the relationship between human and structural capital and the firm's financial capital. He realized that in order to be commercially successful in the long term, the first two capitals must focus on customer-related interests. In so doing, the firm creates a stock of capital around its customers, which St. Onge dubbed customer capital. (St. Onge defines structural capital in largely the same way that this book defines intellectual assets; see definition later in this appendix.) The St. Onge model shows that long-term profits are created at the confluence between human, structural, and customer capital.

Patrick Sullivan—The focus of Sullivan's work has been the extraction of value from IC. As one of the founders of the ICM Gathering, Sullivan has encouraged companies and individuals involved with value extraction to share information and to jointly develop decision processes, methods, and systems that produce practical results. This book is one of the outcomes of that approach. He has been closely associated with the ICM model of a knowledge firm, which was formulated at the first Gathering meeting using much of his thinking as its basis.

Thomas Stewart—Stewart began his association with intellectual capital when, as a feature writer for *Fortune* magazine, he wrote a brief article in 1991 about new ideas in business. That led to a longer story, which became "Brainpower," published in 1992. Stewart's interest in knowledge management led him to write "Intellectual Capital," which appeared in 1994. Stewart has become one of the most visible spokespersons for the field of intellectual capital management and continues to write articles that focus on the brainpower and knowledge management themes he has done so much to popularize. Now a member of the board of editors of *Fortune* magazine, Stewart published a book, *Intellectual Capital— The New Wealth of Organizations* (Doubleday) in 1997.

Gordon Petrash—Originally trained as an architect, Petrash joined Dow in 1986 as a development manager for construction materials. After successes in both construction materials management and in managing Dow's Styrofoam films business, he was asked to create an intellectual asset management function to identify innovations or ideas that might have been overlooked by the corporation and bring them to commercialization if possible. Petrash developed an intellectual asset vision and implementation model, including approaches and tools to enable the company to maximize the value of its existing portfolio of intellectual assets. The success of this work led Dow to expand his responsibilities. Petrash was Dow's Director of Intellectual Capital/Knowledge Management. Since 1998 he has been a partner with PriceWaterhouseCoopers, specializing in consulting on intellectual assets with an emphasis on tax donations.

Leif Edvinsson—As Corporate Director of Intellectual Capital at Skandia AFS, a Swedish insurance company, Edvinsson was responsible for creating ways to describe what Skandia called "the hidden values" and develop an intellectual capital management model for the firm. As one of the best-known spokespersons for intellectual capital management, Edvinsson built upon the concept pioneered by Sveiby of reporting on external capital. Skandia has now issued some six intellectual supplements to its annual financial reports, outlining the firm's intellectual capital and the ways in which this hidden value is used for the benefit of customers and shareholders.

Baruch Lev—Currently a professor at the Stern School of Management at New York University, Lev first began his research into valuing intangibles in the early 1990s as a colleague of David Teece's at UC Berkeley's Haas School of Business. Lev's work focuses on quantifying the value of intangibles and correlating those values with financial measures observable in the capital markets.

Another view of the evolution of thought on intellectual capital management shows the relationships among the several key players. This view, presented in Exhibit A.7, shows the evolution of their thinking in the areas of value creation and value extraction.

The ICM Gathering

In the autumn of 1994, Gordon Petrash of Dow Chemical, Leif Edvinsson of Skandia, and I were concerned that despite how much we thought we knew about intellectual capital, there might be a considerable amount that we didn't know. In an effort to learn more about intellectual capital and how it might be managed, we decided to call together *all* of the companies in the world that we knew were actively managing their intellectual assets and ask each company to describe its view of IC and ICM. By looking at "the elephant" from their different perspectives we expected to see more clearly what the elephant looked like.

We invited representatives of these companies to meet in Berkeley in January 1995. The participants included Dow, DuPont, Hewlett-Packard, Hughes Space and Communications, Hoffman LaRoche, Skandia, and the Law & Economics Consulting Group (with which I was then affiliated).

The meeting participants set as their purpose to define the term intellectual capital and to determine how it is managed, at least for those companies attending the meeting. At the end of an opening round of show-and-tell it was clear that each company defined intellectual capital differently and managed its resources in this area differently as well. At the end of the day we were all perplexed and troubled; no common pattern seemed to be emerging. The next morning we met again and, using some group-discussion techniques as well as lots of blackboard drawings, slowly came to realize that we were, in fact, all talking about the same thing but using the same terms with different definitions. To facilitate meaningful dialogue, we proceeded to develop a common set of definitions and descriptions.

Having agreed to meet for one day and a half, by noon on the second day the excitement level in the room was almost electric;

no one wanted the meeting to end. We agreed to meet again four months later to continue the conversation. We have continued to meet every four months since. The group formally calls itself The ICM (Intellectual Capital Managers) Gathering. The members of the Gathering agree a priori on the "hot topics" to be featured at each forthcoming meeting, speakers are invited, and hotels are booked.

Meetings usually begin slowly, with show-and-tell around the table concerning the agreed topic. On the first day, participants jot down issues and potential topics for the next morning's discussions. At the beginning of the second day, a long list of potential discussion topics is quickly winnowed down to the two or three "hottest." The discussions that follow take on a life and an energy of their own. In the room are people who are among the most knowledgeable in the world about the practice of managing intellectual capital. They share a collective knowledge that is probably unequaled. When this collective knowledge is focused on topics of mutual interest and importance, the result represents the very best thinking possible.

The interest and energy generated by being in the company of others who were interested in extracting value from intellectual capital led me (with several others) to form The ICM Group, a consulting company focused on developing innovative methods, procedures, and techniques for companies to use in extracting the most profits possible from their intellectual capital. The number of companies interested in learning more about this new field of management continues to grow. Their interest is in learning how to make more profits from their existing intellectual capital, and how to use their intellectual capital as a basis for creating the profits, both now and in the future.

By virtue of their early commitment and head start, Gathering companies are perhaps five years ahead of others in their thinking on technology commercialization. This book contains many of the lessons these companies have learned, from themselves and from one another. These lessons are not proprietary or secret. The Gathering companies realize it is in their self-interest to have more companies learning and sharing how to manage and profit from intellectual capital.

MANAGEMENT CONCEPTS

The Importance of Context

Value, a concept addressed throughout this book, is discussed from the perspective of the economist. Economists view value as the sum of a stream of benefits (or income) stretching into the future, summed and discounted to a net present value in dollars. Yet value has meaning for many others besides economists. Consider a painting of some fishing boats in a tropical harbor. To an interior decorator, the painting might have value if its colors complement the color scheme of a room. To an artist, the painting's value might be related to its creator, the technique used to paint it, or its perspective on the subjects. To an art dealer, its value might lie in the price it can command, and to the owner its value might be sentimental, because it was painted by Aunt Maisie on her trip to Tahiti. In all of these situations, the value depends upon who determines it. In other words, the value depends on the values of the valuer.

If there can be as many views of value for a tangible object like a painting, then what must be the case with an intangible? Its value too depends on who determines its value and in what context. For example, a plastic bottle filled with water and sitting at the bottom of a lake in rainy England might have little value; indeed it might be seen as a nuisance to the pool owner. That same container of water in the middle of the Sahara could have enormous value.

The relative value placed on innovative ideas is largely dependent upon the firm's view of itself, and upon the reality of the marketplace. Put another way, each firm exists within a context that shapes the firm's view of what is or is not of value.

Context may be defined as the firm's internal and external realities. Internal realities concern direction, resources, and constraints. They define the firm's strengths and weaknesses as well as its capabilities for competing in its external world. The external realities concern opportunities and threats and focus on the fundamental forces affecting the long-term viability of the industry as well as the immediate opportunities available to the firm.

Internal Dimensions of Context

Questions asked to determine the internal context center on direction, resources, and constraints. What business is the firm really in? How does the firm define its business? What are the firm's strengths and weaknesses? What are the levers to pull for growth? What strategies are available? What strategies has the firm selected? Why? What is the firm's current performance against goal? Is this performance acceptable?

External Dimensions of Context

Questions asked to determine the external context center on identifying the fundamental forces affecting the industry as well as the immediate opportunities available in the firm's marketplace. What are the major environmental forces affecting success in this business (e.g., economic, governmental, technological, sociological, political)? What is the firm's market? How is it changing (getting larger, declining, etc.)? Who are the firm's competitors? What are their strengths and weaknesses? What are the best market strategies?

Companies that manage their intellectual capital successfully realize that two fundamental elements of the context are particularly useful to know: *values* and *vision*. In that regard, two short mantras are useful in determining the context for valuing something:

1. Values $\Rightarrow$ Value $\Rightarrow$ Valuation
2. Vision $\Rightarrow$ Strategy $\Rightarrow$ Value

The underlying idea of number 1 is that the values of a firm are major determinants of what it holds to be of value. Once the firm's values are known, it becomes possible to know how a firm should value an item. Number 2 is based on similar but different reasoning—that if a firm has a vision of what it wants to become, then it will be able to know whether an item (of intellectual capital) might help move it toward that vision. If an item would be helpful, then it has value for the firm. If it has no usefulness in moving the firm toward its vision or objectives, then it has little value. Combining the two mantras suggests that understanding the company's vision as well as its values may be basic to understanding the value of intellectual capital to a firm. (See Exhibit A.8.)

The following two sections expand on the meaning of vision and values, how they are used, and why a firm's vision and values are basic to understanding how it values its intellectual capital.

Vision

A firm's vision describes the firm as it wishes to be in the future. The vision often provides the standard against which a new innovation is measured: will the innovation help the firm achieve its long-term vision? Can the firm capitalize on or

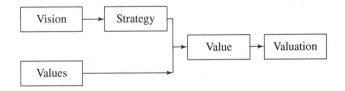

Exhibit A.8   Vision, Values, and the Value Relationship

Source: Patrick H. Sullivan, *Profiting from Intellectual Capital: Extracting Value from Innovation.* Copyright © 1998 by John Wiley & Sons, Inc. Reprinted by permission of John Wiley & Sons, Inc.

somehow use the innovation to improve internal operations, how it is viewed by the marketplace, or the list of innovations to commercialize? Will it lead to increased sales? Will it improve internal efficiency? Will it improve the firm's ability to develop new innovations? Are these things important to the firm? If so, the idea has value. If not, then the idea has little value.

Perhaps one of the most famous and ultimately successful vision statements was made by President John F. Kennedy in his speech to Congress in May 1961 when he said, "I believe that this nation should commit itself to achieving the goal, before this decade is out, of landing a man on the moon and returning him safely to the earth."

Despite the power of such statements, most organizations struggle with two important things: determining what they want to become in the future and determining what to do in order to achieve the vision. Before the mid-1980s, management literature did not effectively differentiate between these two ideas. Firms often confused long-term objectives (vision) with the steps to be taken to get there (strategy), but by the mid-1980s it was becoming clear to practitioners and theorists alike that the methods for determining strategic direction should be refined. The basic tenet of this emerging school of thought was that companies could decide in advance what they wished their future to be and then create that future themselves.

Professor Stan Davis at Boston University said it well when he described the process as making a decision about what the firm wished to become in the future, and then managing the *beforemath* of that decision.

Strategic vision and strategy for a firm may be selected in a number of ways: *inspiration* or the brilliant vision of the leader, *accommodation* among competing political factions, *rational choice* after careful study, or *default* (the path of least resistance). These and many other general categorizations describe the ways organizations arrive at their business strategy for the future. The rational-choice style, espoused by many but practiced by few, is the most difficult and complex approach, yet it offers the greatest reward. This appendix discusses the use of strategic vision in the rational-choice approach and attempts to explain the advantages of this method.

There are good reasons given by companies for the approach they adopt. For example, companies arriving at their strategic direction by default find themselves on a trajectory that seems to produce results and then stay with it. After all, the argument goes, it's working well for us so far. Still other companies turn to their CEO for that inspiring view of the future that will define what the firm will become. Unfortunately, most CEOs are mortal and not gifted with the ability to see the future clearly. Nor are they necessarily able to divine a successful strategy that will carry the firm toward the achievement of the vision. Still other companies, probably organizations that are more people-oriented, will go through major internal debates, with strong positions becoming established and win-lose situations being developed between the leaders of what often become warring camps. Companies such as these usually end up with a no-decision strategy (default) or an accommodation strategy that suboptimizes the firm's capabilities and future.

The importance of a well-conceived and well-articulated vision of the future is perhaps the most important piece of intellectual capital a firm can develop. Once known and widely acknowledged, such a view of the future allows employees at all levels of the firm to know whether an idea or an activity makes sense to pursue. It helps people know which path to take.

Strategy Development

Experience has shown that firms with a desire to shape their own future can do so successfully. The essence of a firm's ability to determine its future is the effective use of strategic choice. In the context of strategy development, choice means that a firm can identify a set of significantly different yet equally desirable futures for itself. These futures represent the choices available to the firm. With these choices in mind, the firm can decide which future to bring into being. This process of developing control of the future through choice rests upon two fundamental beliefs: The future of a firm can be knowable in advance, and a firm can take actions that will bring that desired future into being.

The process of thinking into the future (developing plans and strategies) is a well-known one, and there is general agreement that it flows along a spectrum of planning activity as outlined in Exhibit A.9. This spectrum divides strategy development into two distinct segments: *strategic thinking* and *strategic planning*.

Strategic thinking is a component of the strategic vision and may result, eventually, in a strategic plan. For organizations beginning the strategic thinking process, the starting point is usually the development of a broad mission statement, which outlines why the firm exists. This is followed by a description of what the firm wishes to be in the future (the vision). Next comes a definition of the steps, both giant steps (objectives) and near-term or one-year steps (goals) for achieving the vision. Only at this point does a strategy, or the plan for achieving the vision, objectives, and goals, emerge. These steps are collectively the contents of the strategic thinking end of the strategy development spectrum. They are followed by strategic planning.

Thinking strategically requires developing a mindset that focuses on the long-range view of the company, its constituencies as well as its micro and macro environments, in order to describe what it can become in the future. Strategic thinking involves:

- Describing the company as it exists, and describing the desired form of the company in the future.

Mission	Vision	Objectives	Goals	Issues	Alternatives	Decision	Action Plans

Strategic Thinking

Strategic Planning

Exhibit A.9   The Strategy Development Spectrum

Source: Patrick H. Sullivan, *Profiting from Intellectual Capital: Extracting Value from Innovation.* Copyright © 1998 by John Wiley & Sons, Inc. Reprinted by permission of John Wiley & Sons, Inc.

- Identifying the growth steps necessary to get from here to there.
- Developing a schedule for taking each step.

Strategic planning requires identifying the major obstacles to achieving the firm's targets and milestones and developing action plans to reach them within the available resources of time, money, manpower, and facilities.

Defining a Vision

A strategic vision is *a set of operationally meaningful statements describing the organization as it wishes to be in the future*. It is more specific than a mission statement, which sets forth objectives in broad business terms. It differs from a strategic plan in that the latter describes specific steps leading to the achievement of long-term goals. The strategic vision focuses on operational activities that will make the organization into what it wishes to become, leaving the matter of how to later plan to individual initiative. The vision selected must be feasible as well as compatible with the organization's mission and its values.

Another way to understand strategic vision is to focus on the reasons for creating one. Here are some observations about what a well-conceived and broadly accepted strategic vision can do for an organization:

1. The vision provides strategic meaning for the organization. Vision permits the organization to focus its energies, for if everything is important, nothing is important. Vision differentiates foreground from background. Because the foreground acquires meaning only in relation to the background, an important part of vision development is to say what is excluded from the vision.

2. The vision provides a common definition of subjective social reality for the organization's members. It defines a

vocabulary and a framework for discussing alternative plans, actions, and potential outcomes. It symbolizes an infrastructure of values, culture, and context that helps individual actors relate to one another and to the more abstract organization of which they are a part.

3. The vision provides a reference point for managing the organization's *beforemath*. It pulls people toward the desired future, reducing the need for formal directives.

4. The vision is most important when dimensions of the proposed change are quite large, when the change involves organizational values, culture, or structure, and the time to adjust is long. It provides a continuing focal point as people and conditions change during the implementation of the strategic plan.

A final word on visioning. Many organizations believe they have a vision for the future, but few have visions that are strategically helpful. In order to be helpful, a vision must state what the company wishes to become in operational terms, not how it intends to get there. It is very important that visions describe the future state in a way that allows progress toward it to be measured. (Otherwise, the use of terms such as "best" or "preferred" or "number one" are meaningless.) With a well-articulated vision for the future, and a firm grasp on where the company is now, any firm is in a position to make the strategic decisions that will help it achieve its vision.

Values

The values of the firm represent the consensus beliefs of its members. The sum of these views, the collective values of the firm, determine the world view held by the employees. Values drive the day-to-day decision-making of employees. If the values of the employees differ from those of the executive management, the employees will be unlikely to effectively implement the firm's strategic plan.

Values are ideals that shape and give significance to our lives. They are reflected in the priorities we choose, the decisions we make, and the actions we take. Values are ideals that individuals select and use as the basis for many decisions in day-to-day life. As decision prioritizers, values are reflected in behavior. As ideals, they provide meaning for people's lives. Values are also measurable. Using a list of 125 values that are important to individuals, teams, and organizations, and that are inherent or referred to in an organization's documents, Dr. Brian Hall of Values Technology, Inc. provides a common language or yardstick for discussing values and the issues they influence.

Value

Value is a concept that has many meanings, each of which may apply in a narrow or unique set of circumstances. For example, the value of a piece of rental property may be assessed somewhat differently by a seller, a potential buyer, an insurance company, a tax assessor, the executor of an estate containing the property, a government entity considering taking possession by eminent domain, and a potential mortgage lender. The value of an item depends primarily on the needs of the person or organization that will be using it. Defining and measuring the value of intellectual capital is discussed extensively throughout this book, and also in the sections that follow.

In the business context, value measurements are used for decision-making. The value of an intangible or a piece of intellectual capital is often the basis for deciding whether to invest further in developing the intangible, to continue holding it, or to sell it. This kind of value measurement may be called economic; that is, it is a measure of the utility the intangible brings to the firm.

In measuring economic value to the firm, it is necessary to have a reference point to use as the basis for measurement. In the case of ongoing enterprises such as knowledge companies, a particularly useful reference point is the firm's vision of itself in the future. This vision, as well as its strategy for achieving the vision, may be used as the basis for measuring the utility or value of intangibles such as intellectual capital. If an intellectual asset such as an idea, a patent, or a process can assist the company in implementing its strategy or achieving its vision, then it has value to the firm. The amount of value depends on the degree to which the intellectual asset enables the strategy or vision.

We have already defined intellectual capital as knowledge that can be converted into profits. We have also shown that intellectual capital includes the company's tacit and explicit knowledge, its know-how and uncodified knowledge, as well as its written plans, procedures, patents, and customer lists. This section of the appendix discusses basic concepts about value: what it is, how the concepts of value and intellectual capital relate, and how companies can convert their intellectual capital into profits.

Value extraction from intellectual capital, unlike value extraction from intellectual assets or intellectual properties, is fundamentally a strategic activity. Firms that actively extract value from their intellectual capital do so in two ways. First, they internally align their intellectual capital with the firm's vision and strategy in order to ensure that both their intellectual and structural capital are focused on achieving the right goal. Second, they report to the external world on the firm's intellectual capital, both the amount of it and the company's ability to leverage it in the marketplace.

Strategic Alignment of Intellectual Capital

The alignment of the firm's intellectual capital with its vision and strategy is a powerful idea. Indeed, the idea of alignment underlies virtually all management theories, concepts, fads, and fashions. The power of the concept of alignment is that companies can focus their resources and activities on a set of objectives for the purpose of achieving them faster or without unnec-essary effort.

Intellectual capital management is an integral part of creating the future of the firm. Although its intellectual property compo-nent is used, and useful, in generating current profits, its major utility is in making the future happen. Alignment of the firm's intellectual capital and strategy requires the presence of a well-articulated and well-understood vision. As Exhibit A.10 shows, the concept of alignment is a simple one.

A company with a well-defined vision of the future and a well-conceived and executed strategy can define the roles its intellectual capital could play in helping it to achieve the vision through the strategy. The roles for IC tend to fall into one of two areas: value creation or value extraction. Companies that have defined the roles for IC can then audit their current actual use of

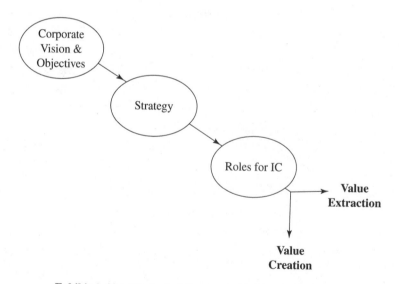

Exhibit A.10   Strategic Alignment of Intellectual Capital

Source: Patrick H. Sullivan, *Profiting from Intellectual Capital: Extracting Value from Innovation.* Copyright © 1998 by John Wiley & Sons, Inc. Reprinted by permission of John Wiley & Sons, Inc.

intellectual capital to determine how well it aligns with the rules defined for it. The degree to which the current use is not consistent with the desired use is the degree of misalignment.

Firms that wish to alter the view of themselves that is presented to the outside world, particularly where the external view does not include an appreciation of the knowledge content of the firm's activities, are increasingly considering reporting publicly on their intellectual capital. At this writing, several Swedish firms have done so. In 1989, WM-data began publishing external reports of its intellectual capital, based on the model developed by Karl-Eric Sveiby. Skandia AFS, a finance and insurance company, published an intellectual capital supplement to its 1994 annual financial report. Shortly thereafter, the price of Skandia's stock rose by some 40 percent.

In the United States there has been a sharp increase in the interest in external reports of intellectual capital. In 1996 the Securities and Exchange Commission sponsored a symposium to discuss the needs and concerns surrounding such reporting. As a direct outcome of that meeting, New York University founded the Center for Research in Measurement of Intangible Assets headed by Professor Baruch Lev, a professor of accounting. In 1997 think tanks and other organizations nationwide held numerous unofficial meetings and discussions about intellectual capital measurement and reporting issues.

The issues underlying external reporting of intellectual capital involve measurement. Of particular interest to the Securities and Exchange Commission, it is important that intellectual capital be valued according to some consistent and agreed-upon measurements; and people outside the company must trust that the measurements are accurate and relevant to their needs.

But measurement issues extend beyond questions of value. Which measures of intellectual capital are best depends on the context of a firm's own circumstances and management needs. It is not productive to discuss the measurement of intangibles such as intellectual capital without first understanding the context within which the company manages its intellectual capital.

Lacking context, it is impossible to assess whether any measure of IC has meaning for the firm.

Describing and Measuring Intellectual Capital

Generally, three different groups have an interest in describing and measuring intellectual capital. One group is knowledge companies themselves, whose employees must manage these intangibles. As yet, they have inadequate methods for measuring either the stocks of intellectual capital at their firms or, more important, the changes in those stocks that result from management efforts. The company managers need operating measurements of intellectual capital, leading toward what amounts to an intellectual asset operating statement.

Another group is the financial community. An increasing number of knowledge firms (those whose major assets are intellectual and not tangible) are valued highly in the stock market on the basis of the market's perception of each firm's intellectual capital. But, lacking any systematic or common ways of measuring intellectual capital or its value, it is difficult for the members of this group to determine whether the investing public is well served by its perceptions of value. The financial interest group wants to see intangible assets capitalized in a standard and reliable way: on an intangible balance sheet, where the intellectual assets are measured in dollar terms and the valuation methods are credible.

A third group consists of macro-economists whose interest is knowing whether firms' existing use of intellectual capital resources is economically sound for the country. Their need is for data from companies on their intellectual capital that will allow them to conduct analyses of those companies at the national accounts level.

These interest groups have very different reasons for wanting to measure intellectual capital; and their different reasons, while not incompatible with one another, are not likely to measure exactly the same things.

The Relationships Between Measures

When developing a capability for managing intellectual capital, the firm must ask what business objectives it wishes to accomplish and how its intellectual capital supports the achievement of those objectives. Which pools of intellectual capital does management wish to change? How does it wish to change them? Over what time period should the change take place? The answers to these questions allow the firm to decide how to measure and monitor such changes.

Events occurring inside a company are not independent. Different pieces of a firm's intellectual capital affect one another. Discovering and understanding these relationships is our final goal. For example, companies track annual expenditures such as advertising to understand the relationship between advertising dollars spent and increases in consumer awareness and, ultimately, increased sales revenue.

Our goal in measuring intellectual capital is to understand the relationships between and among IC components. Once the relationships are made explicit, it is much easier to manage intellectual capital to obtain the corporate vision, strategy, and objectives.

Factors Affecting Measurement

There are a series of factors that determine what a firm wishes to measure and what measures it selects. For example, recall the discussion on aligning intellectual capital with the vision and strategy of the firm. In the course of such an alignment, the firm determines the various roles played by intellectual capital in that firm. These roles are further subdivided into value creation and value extraction. In the case of value extraction, a further division may be required to elucidate what the firm wishes to accomplish through value extraction, thereby beginning the process of determining what it wishes to measure.

Once the roles for value extraction are defined, the firm can develop a series of objectives for value extraction activities.

Defining objectives allows the firm to make explicit what it wishes to accomplish through its management of IC. Further, the accomplishments, once defined in IC terms, allow IC goals and targets to be established. The creation of specific goals and targets for IC will determine what managers decide to measure and what they monitor over time.

Dimensions of Measurement

Once the "what" of measurement has been determined, it becomes necessary to decide how the measurement will be made. In making this determination several dimensions of measurement need to be considered.

Measures can be either qualitative or quantitative. Qualitative measures can be either value-based (e.g., determining the quality) or vector-based (are we moving forward or backward?). Quantitative measures can be either financial or nonfinancial. Again, all contain appropriate measures that depend on what is being measured and why.

Most people think of measurement in quantitative terms: feet, time, weight, dollars, and so forth. Such measurements allow us to determine where we have been, where we are going (in terms of distance and time), and where we are today in a physical sense. For companies, measurement has traditionally been centered on quantitative output, in particular, dollars and time. Quantitative measures provide a numeric, and largely financial, snapshot of the firm. What has been the net profit for the past three quarters? How much have expenses grown as a percentage of revenues over the past two years? Here the emphasis has been largely on financial output, which was designed to provide accurate historical information.

Qualitative measures provide a sense of what is happening. Qualitative measures provide information about the vector of change rather than the speed of change. Often when we work with companies to create an intellectual property management system, one of the first things they tell us is the number of patents in their portfolio, but the qualitative measures of the portfolio are frequently more relevant. For example, within a firm's patent portfolio, does the firm have patents that are of crown jewel quality? Does it have vanity patents with little value? Qualitative measures tend to be very context-specific. Hewlett-Packard and Rockwell, for example, define crown jewel-quality patents in different ways because the definitions are tied to the different strategies of each firm.

Creating an Internal Capability to Manage Intellectual Capital

The two different kinds of knowledge companies, technology companies and service companies, share an interest in managing their intellectual capital. In both cases, the management of IC is a strategic activity that requires the alignment of intellectual capital with the company's vision and strategy, as well as external positioning of the firm.

Strategic value extraction by knowledge companies is typically focused more on the firm's future than on its immediate needs. The firm's strategic vision and positioning are usually based on the current or intended intellectual capital capabilities of the firm. Strategic alignment usually involves focusing the firm's intellectual capital resources on the activities that will enable the strategy and move the firm toward its vision. Both strategic positioning and strategic alignment involve managing the firm's intellectual and structural resources to enable the rapid and efficient achievement of the vision, and reporting externally to the financial markets on the firm's strategic uses of intellectual capital and the implications of these uses on the firm's long-term ability to create value for shareholders.

A Framework for Managing Intellectual Capital

For many years knowledge companies were not differentiable from other kinds of businesses. They used the same standard business model as other firms, managed and reported on their physical assets in the same ways, and used the same protocols for financial reporting and internal accounting. That standard business model is useful, largely because it is well understood and widely accepted, but it emerged when most companies were largely concerned about physical and financial assets. Intellectual assets had not yet become a factor to contend with in business.

With the rise in importance of intellectual capital, the management of intangibles, and the emergence of knowledge companies, the intellectual capital framework has emerged as a model for companies to consider. Looking at a knowledge company through the intellectual capital framework is like tilting the company 30 degrees on one of its axes and 15 degrees on another. The view that this new perspective provides is different from the standard business model and also complementary. It provides knowledge companies with yet one more tool for managing their resources to produce larger profits.

At this stage in its evolution, the IC framework consists of several elements:

- The company vision for its future, and its business strategy for achieving the vision
- A definition of the role intellectual capital is to play in enabling the vision and the strategy
- A definition of the roles of value creation and value extraction
- Value extraction mechanisms
- Systems for routinely administering, managing, and directing the firm's intellectual capital:
  - Management and information systems
  - Decision processes
  - Work processes
  - Databases

In addition to the generally accepted business decisions and approaches, it shows that the alignment of intellectual capital, its full utilization, and the full extraction of the value it creates can produce more powerful market presence and more profits.

The concepts and definitions discussed in this appendix form the major elements of an IC framework, or a way of defining and looking at a company that differs from traditional views. Intellectual capital (and its major subcomponents of people and paper) and structural capital are the fundamental elements of the IC framework in a knowledge company. The economist's concepts of complementary business assets and sources of value help a firm to chart a path toward maximizing the value of the firm's intellectual capital. The commercialization decision process, which demonstrates the relationships among protection, complementary assets, and the conversion mechanism alternatives, allow a firm to project the flow from tacit knowledge to codified knowledge to protected knowledge to complementary assets to conversion to profits.

The IC framework as described so far provides a different perspective for managers interested in developing profits from a firm's innovations, but it leaves unanswered questions about how the firm goes about accomplishing what the framework suggests. The "how" of IC management is covered in this book in discussions of intellectual capital management, intellectual assets, and intellectual properties. The "how" questions require the development of systems, decision processes, work processes, and databases. They also require knowledge about how intellectual capital elements are defined, described, and measured. Further, they require more information about how the elements of intellectual capital relate to the firm's bottom line. This appendix has dealt almost exclusively with the concepts underlying intellectual capital and its management, while the remainder of the book is devoted to how intellectual capital is defined, measured, managed, and monitored, as well as how to demonstrate its relationship to the firm's bottom line

Bibliography

Boulton, R., E. Ginault, and B. Libert. *Value Dynamics*. New York: HarperCollins, January 2000.

Brison, G., L.R. Hood, and G. Beebower. "Determinants of Portfolio Performance." *Financial Analysts Journal,* July–August, 1986, pp. 39–44.

Davis, J. "Using Your IP to Increase Shareholder Value." *Patent Yearbook 1998.* London: Euromoney Publications PLC, 1998.

Edvinsson, L., and P. Sullivan. "Developing a Model for Managing Intellectual Capital." *European Management Journal* 14, no. 4 (August 1996).

Itami, H., and T. W. Roehl. *Mobilizing Invisible Assets.* Cambridge, Mass.: Harvard University Press, 1987.

Nonaka, I., and H. Takeuchi. *The Knowledge Creating Company.* New York: Oxford University Press, 1995.

Parr, R. L., and P. H. Sullivan. *Technology Licensing: Corporate Strategies for Maximizing Value.* New York: John Wiley & Sons, Inc., 1996.

Petrash, G. "Dow's Journey to a Knowledge Value Management Culture." *European Management Journal* 14, no. 4 (August 1996).

Porter, M. E. *Competitive Strategy.* New York: Free Press, 1980.

————. "What Is Strategy?" *Harvard Business Review* (Nov.–Dec. 1996): 61–78.

Prahalad, C. K., and G. Hame. "The Core Competence of the Corporation." *Harvard Business Review* 68, no. 3: 79–91.

St.-Onge, H. "Intellectual Capital as a Business Reality," unpublished presentation, 1996.

Shapiro, C. "The Theory of Business Strategy." *RAND Journal of Economics* 20, no. 1: 125–137.

Stewart, T. *Intellectual Capital:* "Brainpower." *Fortune*, June 3, 1991, p. 44.

————. "Your Company's Most Valuable Asset: Intellectual Capital." *Fortune*, October 3, 1994 (cover story).

————. *The New Wealth of Organizations.* New York: Doubleday, 1997.

Sullivan, P. H. "Extracting Value from Intellectual Capital: Policy and Practice." In *Capital for Our Time: The Economic, Management and Legal Challenge of Intellectual Capital.* Stanford, Calif.: Hoover Institution Press, Stanford University, 1999.

————. "Profiting from Intellectual Capital." *Journal of Knowledge Management,* Volume 3, Issue 2, 1998.

————. *Profiting from Intellectual Capital: Extracting Value from Innovation.* New York: John Wiley & Sons, Inc., 1998.

————. "Capturing Value from Intellectual Property." In *Hidden Value: Profiting from the Intellectual Property Economy,* P. Berman, ed, June 1999.

Sullivan, P. H., and J. O'Shaughnessy. "Valuing Knowledge Companies." *Les Nouvelles,* June 1999.

Sullivan, P. H., and R. Sproule. "Integrating Licensing at Boeing: Two Views of a Benchmark Effort." *Les Nouvelles,* September 1999.

Sullivan, S. "Insights into Commercializing Technology." *Les Nouvelles*, March 1993, pp. 30–35.

Sveiby, K.-E. *The New Organizational Wealth: Managing and Measuring Knowledge-Based Assets.* San Francisco: Berrett-Koehler Publishers, 1997.

Teece, D. "Profiting from Technological Innovation: Implications for Integration, Collaboration, Licensing and Public Policy." *Research Policy* 15 (1986): 285–305.

Teece, D., G. Pisano, and A. Shuen. "Dynamic Capabilities and Strategic Management." *Strategic Management Journal* 18, no. 7 (1997): 509–533.

INDEX